MW00531976

Law and Society
Recent Scholarship

Edited by Melvin I. Urofsky

A Series from LFB Scholarly

The Juror Factor
Race and Gender in America's Civil Courts

Sean G. Overland

LFB Scholarly Publishing LLC
El Paso 2009

Library of Congress Cataloging-in-Publication Data

Overland, Sean G., 1973-
The juror factor : race and gender in America's civil courts / Sean G. Overland.
p. cm. -- (Law and society)
Includes bibliographical references and index.
ISBN 978-1-59332-328-8 (alk. paper)
1. Jury--United States--Psychology. 2. Jury--United States--Decision making. 3. Trial practice--United States--Psychological aspects. 4. Verdicts--United States--Psychological aspects. I. Title.
KF8972.O94 2009
347.73'752--dc22

2008043884

ISBN 978-1-59332-328-8

Printed on acid-free 250-year-life paper.

Manufactured in the United States of America.

To my Dad, who is always up for
a good debate about juries.

Table of Contents

List of Tables

Acknowledgments

For their helpful comments on earlier drafts of this book, I would like to thank Alison Anderson of the UCLA Law School and David Sears, Lynn Vavreck and in particular Karen Orren of the UCLA Department of Political Science. Many thanks go to Larry Mattson and Drury Sherrod for their continuing support and guidance. Thanks also to Eric Gober for his careful proofreading and conscientious collection of much of the data. And thanks to Roberta O'Donnell for teaching me everything I know about statistical software.

Thanks to my dear friends H. Robert Baker, John T. Eldevik, Mary B. McThomas, Elizabeth A. Stein and Gabriel K. Wolfenstein for their helpful advice on all things professional and personal.

And last but certainly not least, thanks to my wonderful family and in particular my parents, Eric and Marjorie Overland and my wonderful siblings Henrik, Liz, Maryann and Tim.

INTRODUCTION:
Debating the Civil Jury

The civil jury must rank among the most controversial of America's political and legal institutions. To paraphrase Kalvan and Zeisel's ground-breaking work, the jury is a group of people, chosen at random, who are then entrusted with official decision-making powers, yet who make their decisions in secret and with little or no explanation. It is therefore not surprising that the jury has been the subject of both extravagant praise and harsh criticism (Kalven and Zeisel, 1966, pg. 66). Indeed, contemporary critics of the civil justice system decry a "litigation explosion" of "frivolous lawsuits" decided by incompetent, irrational and gullible jurors.[1] Despite this heated rhetoric surrounding the jury, relatively little is known about how civil juries reach their verdicts. Leading jury researchers have claimed that, "the study of civil jury decision making is still in its infancy" (Hastie, Schkade and Payne, 1998, pg. 287). This book will attempt to contribute to our understanding of how civil juries reach their verdicts. A better understanding of how juries work may also speak to contemporary debates over the merits of the American civil justice system.

THE FUNCTIONS OF THE CIVIL JURY

The controversy over the civil jury stems in part from the difficult decisions juries are asked to make. The civil jury faces questions no elected body would want to answer. For example, how much should a person be compensated for losing a loved one because of the negligence of another? What is a permanent injury worth? What if a plaintiff is partially responsible for his own injury? Should that plaintiff still receive compensation? In short, how does one translate misfortune into money? There are no good answers to these questions, but the civil jury must make them nonetheless.

Adding to the controversy surrounding the civil jury is its highly democratic nature. Over the past century, the qualifications for jury service in this country have become increasingly easy to meet, with almost all citizens over the age of eighteen now eligible to serve, as long as they are not a felon or mentally incompetent.[2] The broad population from which juries are selected has led critics to claim that citizens drawn from the public at large are ill-qualified to sit in judgment of increasingly complicated and important litigation.

The civil jury is also the victim of some slanted media portrayals. A review of news magazines by Bailis and MacCoun (1996) found that stories on civil jury verdicts focused disproportionately on trials that ended with a verdict for the plaintiff. Another study found similar results in newspaper coverage of jury verdicts. Garber and Bower (1999) looked at newspaper coverage of lawsuits against the major auto-makers between 1983 and 1996. During that period, the auto companies won 259 out of 351 trials that ended with a jury verdict, for a success rate of 74%. However, only 9 of those 259 defense verdicts (or 3%) were covered in any of the sixty major newspapers surveyed. Of the 92 plaintiff victories, however, 38 (or 41%) received newspaper coverage. This disproportionate attention is understandable, as plaintiff victories and large side over the other. Thus, the strategic settlement decisions made by civil litigants prior to trial may insure that jurors only hear cases in which their personal beliefs will have the greatest impact on verdicts.

Because juries are likely to hear only very closely-contested cases, one juror may react very differently than another to the same case. Indeed, research has shown that most juries are not unanimous when they begin their deliberations (Kalven and Zeisel, 1966). Because jurors hear the same information and instructions, some juror-level factor must color their judgments. Diamond points out that:

> the evidence presented at trial cannot account for initial disagreements among jurors: all jurors are exposed to the same evidence. The differences in juror reaction must stem from pre-existing differences among the jurors that affect juror responses to the evidence (Diamond, 1990, pg. 178).

In other words, individual jurors may receive and process the same trial evidence very differently.

An influential explanation for why jurors might differ in their interpretation of the evidence is the "story model."[5] The story model focuses on the importance of mental "narratives," or stories, that jurors formulate to make sense of the evidence presented at trial. When confronted with new, unfamiliar or disjointed information, jurors (and human beings in general) often rely on narratives as a cognitive "short-cut" to help them organize that information, fill in any gaps and make decisions. The narratives that jurors use are shaped by the juror's life experiences, attitudes and general beliefs about how the world works. For example, Pennington and Hastie found that when jurors were asked about what they had heard damages awards are exciting and "newsworthy." Defense verdicts, on the other hand, are seen as non-events; the jury has decided that there is nothing wrong with the company's product and that the defendant is not responsible for the plaintiff's injuries. But if one were to estimate the probability of a plaintiff win at trial based solely on the newspaper coverage of the verdicts, one could erroneously conclude that plaintiffs win at trial far more often than they lose, when in fact the exact opposite is true.

Indeed, many reports of the eccentricities of the civil jury are based on anecdotes of large and seemingly inexplicable damages awards. The descriptions of these jury verdicts are often taken out of context or without a full explanation of the evidence presented at trial. Perhaps the most famous example of a "ridiculous" jury award is the story of a woman who spilled McDonald's coffee on herself, sued the fast-food chain, and won a multi-million dollar award. What is not commonly known, however, is the complete story heard by the jury in *Liebeck v. McDonald's* (1994). The jury heard evidence that McDonald's coffee was routinely served at near boiling temperatures, that McDonald's had received hundreds of complaints and reports of injuries caused by its coffee, and that McDonald's had done nothing to alter its practices. The jury also heard that the plaintiff suffered second and third degree burns on her thighs and groin, which required several skin replacement surgeries. The jury found McDonald's partly liable for the plaintiff's injuries, but also placed some of the blame on the plaintiff herself. The jury also wanted to send a message to McDonald's to serve its coffee at safer temperatures and therefore awarded punitive damages in an amount equal to the value of two days of coffee sales at McDonald's restaurants in the United States. In the end, however, the plaintiff saw only a fraction of that money, eventually agreeing to an undisclosed, post-verdict settlement.

Indeed, before one can make claims about how well juries do their job, one must first understand what exactly the jury is asked to do. This is not an easy task, for juries perform several functions. The task most frequently ascribed to the jury is that of a legal fact-finding body. In other words, the civil jury evaluates the competing and conflicting evidence presented at trial and determines what the facts of the dispute are. While some critics have claimed that juries are incapable of performing this function, most studies on juror decision-making have concluded that jurors do a very good job of understanding case evidence and of using that evidence to reach decisions. Summarizing this scholarship, Galanter writes:

> the literature, on the whole, converges on the judgment that juries are fine decision-makers. They are conscientious [and] collectively they understand and recall the evidence as well as judges (Galanter, 1993, pg. 70. See also Robbennolt, 2005).

While it is difficult to say what is or is not a "good" jury verdict, most research on the quality of jury decisions has compared trial verdicts with the decision a judge would have made in the same case. This research has shown that judges and juries agree on the proper verdict in a large majority of cases. Specifically, studies have found that judges agreed with the jury's verdict more than 75% of the time (Kalven and Zeisel, 1966, pg. 56).[3] But if judges and juries agree on case outcomes, why not rely on judges to decide legal disputes and abolish juries altogether? If a judge and jury agree on verdicts in a large majority of cases, presumably the time and expense of summoning and selecting juries could be avoided at almost no cost to the quality of the legal system's judgments.

The problem with such a suggestion is that the theory of the jury embedded within studies of judge-jury similarity—that is, of a simple fact-finding body—relies on but one of the jury's many functions. This one-dimensional view of the jury is problematic, in that verdicts in these studies are evaluated not in terms of their justness or fairness, but in terms of their consistency with what other decision-makers might do under similar situations. Nothing guarantees that these other decision-makers—judges, "blue ribbon" juries of technical experts or professional arbitrators and mediators—are more likely than a jury to reach a "just" decision.

Thus, to fully evaluate and understand the civil jury and its verdicts, one must also recognize that the civil jury does more than simply determine the facts of a case. The jury also represents the values of the community from which it is drawn. As Marianne Constable puts it, "the jury is not simply a procedural device or mechanism for the evaluation of the evidence in a lawsuit. Rather the jury constitutes a practice in which matters of community membership, truth and law are inextricably intertwined" (Constable, 1994, pg. 1). In other words, the jury applies community values and beliefs to the administration of justice. As such, the jury verdict is more than a statement of fact; it is also an expression of the popular will.

Haddon has a similar view of the civil jury, and describes it as a body that not only decides the facts of a case, but that also represents the community and applies its values and standards to the administration of justice. In this broader view of the jury's role, the jury performs a function that no judge could hope to accomplish. The jury represents the will of the people in the judiciary, and sees to it that "we are governed by the spirit of the law and not merely its letter" (Haddon, 1994, pg. 54).

Because the jury performs more than a simple fact-finding function, it is difficult to evaluate all the dimensions of its performance. If, as the evidence suggests, juries are good fact-finders, do juries also accomplish their function as a body representative of the community and its values? And if so, how should we interpret a jury's verdict? If one accepts the jury as speaking for the community in questions of justice, can a verdict, by its very nature, be evaluated in terms of factual "correctness?" As the Latin origin of the word "verdict" is "to speak the truth," a jury may not only determine the facts of a case but may also "speak the truth" about that case. As such, a jury verdict can be no more factually "correct" or "incorrect" than, for example, the results of an election or a popular referendum. In other words, one can disagree with a jury's verdict, and perhaps believe that the verdict is unjust or imprudent, but one can not question its factual correctness, because it is an expression of the popular will. Indeed, if the jury is a body that expresses community values, then its verdicts are in some sense beyond positive evaluation and should be seen instead as normative expressions of political preference (for more on the political role of the civil jury, see Chapman, 2007).

The role of the jury as a political institution widens the debate about its merits. Questions surrounding the jury's political function draw in issues of representation and the diversity of the communities from which juries are drawn. For example, if a jury's verdict reflects the will of the community, might different communities see the same case differently? If so, can a justice system be truly "just" if the same case is decided differently, depending on where it is tried?

Also intimately tied to the jury's political function are questions of race, gender and class. Some observers have suggested that contemporary criticisms of juror competence may be a thinly-veiled attack on the jury's inclusive nature. Dooley (1994) argues that it is no coincidence that criticisms of the jury have increased as juries have come to include large numbers of women and racial minorities. She points out that in the eighteenth and nineteenth centuries when only white males served as jurors, the jury was widely seen as a bastion of justice and an invaluable civic institution. After reforms brought racial minorities and women into the jury box in increasing numbers, the image of the jury as an institution run amok has come to dominate the conventional wisdom. Dooley argues that the contemporary mistrust of the civil jury is in fact a fear of vesting power in the hands of America's increasingly multicultural population.

Debates over the nature and virtue of jury verdicts can also rapidly evolve into questions of fact, truth and knowledge. As discussed above, juries very often decide much more than mere "facts" and are instead making larger judgments about right and wrong. But is there one "truth" about what happened in a civil dispute, or are there many different "truths," each dependent on the individual juror's interpretation of the evidence? Do the "facts" of a case ever speak for themselves, or is the interpretation of those facts influenced by the pre-existing beliefs of the individual jurors? As Constable puts it, "The tension between characterizing the verdict as potentially accurate "fact" and presenting it as a consistent or coherent reflection of public "values" reveals a dilemma whose manifestation pervade much modern thought" (Constable, 1994, pg. 48). Indeed, whether a jury verdict is a statement of fact or an expressions of values is a question underlying much of the research on the American jury. And whether this tension is a fatal flaw in the American justice system, or its greatest virtue, is perhaps the central question surrounding the jury. This book can not hope to address all of these questions. Debates on the nature and desirability of the civil jury can quickly become questions of political representation, business regulation, economic redistribution, social justice, and even the nature of truth itself. It is my hope that the following chapters may speak in some small way to these important questions.

THE PLAN OF THE BOOK

The following chapters explore questions of jurors' race, gender and attitudes, and the effects of those "juror factors" on the American civil justice system. Chapter 1 reviews the literature on juror decision-making. Somewhat surprisingly, the bulk of this scholarship has concluded that juror factors have little effect on trial outcomes. However, many of these studies suffer from methodological short-comings, including, among others, a lack of reliable data on juror decision-making. These problems may have prevented researchers from fully appreciating the effects of juror characteristics on verdicts.

Chapter 2 then re-examines the link between jurors' characteristics and their verdict decisions. Why do jurors who hear the same information in court often disagree on the proper verdict? Litigators have long held that the composition of the jury, such as the race, gender, income and education of the individual jurors, can affect trial outcomes. Is there any truth to these bits of legal folklore or are they simply outdated and ill-informed stereotypes? This chapter will argue that jurors' traits do affect their verdicts in predictable and measurable ways in three different types of civil litigation.

Chapter 3 comments on the Supreme Court's rulings on jury selection procedures. The Court has held for over a century that state actions violate the Equal Protection Clause of the Fourteenth Amendment when they interfere with the race-neutral selection of jurors. In 1986, the Court's ruling in *Batson v. Kentucky* expanded the Court's anti-discrimination efforts by banning peremptory challenges based solely on race. Yet most commentators recognize that race- and gender-based strikes continue in America's courtrooms. This chapter will argue that the *Batson* line of decisions can only be understood by recognizing the effects of juror race and gender in jury trials.

Lastly, a jury verdict is not an individual decision, but rather a product of the jury's group deliberations. Chapter 4 will therefore examine the nature of jury deliberations and the effects of the deliberation process on jury verdicts. An analysis of data drawn from post-trial interviews conducted with jurors from several trials reveals some insights into the nature of the deliberation process, as well as how often jurors change their minds during deliberations and for what reasons.

A brief conclusion will summarize the book's findings and discuss contemporary calls for reform of the American civil justice system.

CHAPTER 1:

What Do We Know About The Juror Factor?

If asked whether the racial or gender composition of a jury might have anything to do with its eventual verdict, most Americans would probably agree that it does. The assumption underlying this opinion is that men and women, blacks and whites, the rich and the poor, may see the world in very different ways and that jurors' differing world views may color their impressions of a case so much so that different jurors may reach very different decisions about a just verdict. Despite this intuition that different people might see the same case differently, most of the academic research on juror decision-making has reached the rather surprising conclusion that jurors' personal characteristics, including their race, gender, socioeconomic status and so on, have relatively little, if anything, to do with their verdicts in most trials.[4]

This chapter will review the literature on juror decision-making and will argue that methodological problems have obscured the link between juror characteristics and verdicts. These problems include 1) a lack of reliable data on jury decision-making in civil trials, 2) the use of inappropriate statistical methods in many studies, 3) a conflation of the decision-making task facing jurors in civil and criminal trials, and 4) a reluctance to acknowledge any relationship between jurors' demographics and their verdicts. These problems have prevented researchers from fully appreciating the relationship between the composition of a jury and its verdict, particularly in civil trials.

THE LITERATURE ON JUROR DECISION-MAKING

A myriad of different factors may affect a juror's verdict decision. Physical evidence, witness testimony, legal instructions, attorney presentations and the attitudes and values of the jurors all shape jurors' views of a case. Research on jury decision-making has demonstrated that, among all of these factors, the most powerful determinant of a jurors' verdict in both civil and criminal cases is the relative strength of the competing evidence (see Hastie, Schkade and Payne, 1998; Visher, 1987 and Kalven and Zeisel, 1966). Several studies have confirmed that the litigant that presents the strongest case is likely to prevail, regardless of the influence of any other factors that might affect jurors' decision making, including the demographic composition of the jury. Michael Saks writes:

> the effects of evidence (and arguments) are considerably more potent than the effects of juror differences. The more evidence, and the more clear the story told by the evidence, the less important are individual differences among jurors, to the point of vanishing (Saks, 1997, pg. 10).

Hastie, Penrod and Pennington concur, and state that:

> Most experimental studies of jury decision making have failed to detect systematic predictors of juror behavior, but they do suggest the strong influence of evidence on decision making (Hastie, Penrod and Pennington, 1983, pg. 126).

Such claims that evidence is important to verdicts are certainly not surprising. However, when evaluating the effects of evidence and the other factors that may influence a juror's verdict, one must take into account the nature of the cases that are most often resolved by a jury trial. The civil disputes decided by jury are by no means a representative sample of all lawsuits. In fact, 98% of all civil claims in this country are resolved prior to trial. In 1995, only 1.8% of all federal civil cases ended in a jury verdict. The percentages were similar in 1990 (2.2%), 1985 (2.3%) and 1980 (2.5%) (Sward, 2001, pg. 13). This high settlement rate is a function of the strategic decisions made by the litigants. Priest and Klein (1984) argue that both sides of a lawsuit have a strong interest in reaching a pre-trial settlement that saves the costs of continued litigation (see also Waldfogel, 1995). Because both sides can anticipate the evidence that will be presented, and can estimate the probability of winning and the expected value of any damages award, most cases settle long before trial. The small percentage of cases that are left to a jury tend to be the most closely contested cases. The outcome of the closely-contested cases, in which both sides have strong evidence to support their claims, is more difficult to predict than a "slam dunk" for one side or the other. Because the outcomes of closely-contested cases are hard for the litigants to predict, they are also hard for the litigants to accurately value, and thus are less likely to settle prior to trial.

Thus, juries tend to hear only the "50-50" cases in which both sides have strong evidence to support their claims. In such closely-contested cases, however, jurors must rely to a greater degree on their own intuitions, experiences and personal judgments when reaching a verdict, because the evidence may not clearly support one

during a trial, jurors did not mechanically regurgitate the evidence. Instead jurors told stories about what they thought had happened in the case. These stories were a product of not only the evidence, but also of jurors' own views of the world. Pennington and Hastie reported that:

> These story explanations may take the form of the subject's personal experience, general attitudes or beliefs, hypothetical self-analogy, or contrary-to-fact reasoning. This category of remarks indicates the source of the juror's story, that is, why certain interpretations of the evidence were believed to be true or plausible and other interpretations were rejected (Pennington and Hastie, 1986, pg. 247).

In other words, the evidence jurors hear in court is filtered through their individual mental narratives, and the judgments jurors reach are determined not only by the evidence, but also by the narratives into which that evidence is organized. In short, "the story the juror constructs determines the juror's decision" (Pennington and Hastie, 1991, pg. 521).

Given that jurors use narratives to organize the evidence presented to them and that these narratives may differ because of jurors' varying life experiences, one would expect to find correlations between juror-level factors and their verdicts. But to what extent do different stories influence verdicts? Saks concedes that:

> Any two people could be socialized into such different world views that they could interpret and respond to the same information quite differently. But the question deserves a more practical frame: How different are the interpretations and judgments of different members of a venire to the same case presentation? (Saks, 1997, pg. 9).

If the differences between jurors' narratives are small, so too would be any differences in their individual verdict preferences. Indeed, as the next section will show, the bulk of the literature suggests that differences between jurors tend to be small and therefore have little or no effect on the outcome of most trials.

Juror Demographics and Verdicts: The Non-Findings

Intuition suggests that a juror's race and gender could have a significant impact on how that person perceives trial evidence. When the media report on the selection of a jury for a high-profile trial, information on the number of women and racial minorities on the jury is almost always included, with the implication that the composition of the jury matters to the outcome of the trial. However, extensive empirical research has attempted to determine the effect of jurors' demographics on their verdicts and a consensus has emerged in the literature that in most cases, no significant relationships exist between jurors' personal characteristics, such as race, income, education or gender, and their verdicts. For example, Shari Diamond's 2006 review of ten common views of the jury reported that, "Demographic characteristics like gender, race and age generally account for very little of the variation in [verdict] response" (Diamond, 2006, pg. 737). Similarly, in their comprehensive review of the jury decision-making literature, Devine, *et al.* concluded that:

> After extensive study, it is now clear that few if any juror characteristics are good predictors of juror verdict preferences. Those characteristics found to be related to juror verdict preferences have tended

> to have weak and inconsistent effects (Devine, *et al.*, 2001, pg. 673).

Saks comes to the same conclusion, arguing that, "even where individual difference variables do predict jurors' preferences, these differences are of a small magnitude" (Saks, 1997, pg. 10). And Hastie, Penrod and Pennington conclude their findings by stating:

> In summary, the relationship is weak between the background characteristics of jurors, such as demography, personality, and general attitudes, and their verdict preferences in typical felony cases (Hastie, Penrod and Pennington, 1983, pg. 149).

These conclusions about the literature are not new. Summarizing the literature as of 1977, Davis, *et al.* complained that, "the inefficacy of individual difference variables, long lamented by small group researchers, continues in jury research" (Davis, Bray and Holt, 1977, pg. 350).

Among the most frequently cited articles on the irrelevance of demographics to juror decision-making is Visher's study of jurors who served on sexual assault trials. She interviewed 340 jurors about the reasons for their verdicts and grouped jurors' remarks about their decisions into categories, such as "the use of a weapon," "physical evidence" and "evidence of force." She also asked the jurors questions about their attitudes toward crime in general, and rape in particular, and she recorded the jurors' demographic information. Visher found that the variables for the juror's description of the evidence presented during the trial "explained" 34% of the variance in jurors' verdict decisions. She also found that "victim and defendant characteristics accounted for another 8% and jurors' characteristics and attitudes only accounted for 2%," of the variance in verdicts (Visher, 1987, pg. 13). From these results, Visher argued that, "research suggests that jurors' personal characteristics are substantively insignificant in affecting trial outcomes" (Visher, 1987, pg. 3).

Most research on juror decision-making focuses on juries hearing criminal cases. However, researchers have concluded that jurors' characteristics have little or no effect on verdicts in civil cases either. Reviewing the literature on jurors' verdicts in civil lawsuits as of 2003, Greene and Bornstein report:

> If they matter at all, individual demographic differences exert a small and inconsistent influence on award values and probably account for a tiny fraction of the variance in assessed damages. Jurors' decision about compensation—like their judgments of a criminal defendant's guilt—apparently cross gender, political and economic lines (Greene and Bornstein, 2003, pg. 87).

After reporting that jurors' demographics had little impact on general damages awards in their study of civil lawsuits, Wissler, Hart and Saks wrote:

> Because a finding that the background characteristics of the decision-makers have little or no impact on their decisions may surprise some readers unacquainted with the relevant literature, it may be worth mentioning that this merely extends a finding now well established elsewhere in the jury decision-making literature. Though most of that research has been on criminal trials, juror socio-demographic characteristics have also been found to play only a modest role in their civil liability verdicts, certainly compared to the dominant impact of evidence and arguments presented in the cases. The present study, along with other recent research,

> suggests that what had been learned about liability verdicts can be extended to damages-relevant responses: individual differences make little difference (Wissler, Hart and Saks, 2000, pg. 805).

Eisenberg and Wells' empirical study of civil damages awards came to the same conclusion. Eisenberg and Wells looked for correlations between the demographics of trial venues and the civil verdicts from courts in those venues. Their analysis revealed that race and other demographic variables had no effect on damages awards. The authors wrote that, "black population percentage does not correlate with award amounts at statistically-significant levels" (Eisenberg and Wells, 2002, pg. 1857). Eisenberg and Wells also found that when looking at the rate at which plaintiffs win trials, "the overall pattern in state trials is one of fairly consistent insignificant correlations between demographic factors and plaintiff trial win rates" (Eisenberg and Wells, 2002, pg. 1863). Eisenberg and Wells conclude that:

> We find little robust evidence that a trial locale's population demographics help explain jury trial outcomes. In tort cases, jury trial awards and plaintiff success rates do not consistently increase significantly with black population percentage (Eisenberg and Wells, 2002, pg. 1869).

Reviewing Eisenberg and Wells' article, Saks concludes that the debate over the effects of juror demographics is all but settled: "In short, it is not news that demographic variables add little to predictions of civil jury verdicts. The Eisenberg and Wells study provides one more such study… (if there is still a debate)" (Saks, 2002, pg. 1882).

Linking Juror Race and Verdicts

Although the bulk of the literature has found little evidence of juror-level effects on verdicts, several studies have hinted that there may yet be connections between juror factors, particularly juror race, and trial outcomes. For example, research on juror decision-making in criminal trials with racial undertones, such as cases in which the victim and the defendant are from different racial backgrounds, has shown that blacks and whites often view the case very differently. This tendency was readily apparent after the "trial of the century" of (black) football star O.J. Simpson for the murder of his (white) wife Nicole and her (white) friend Ron Goldman. When asked in a national opinion poll about their reactions to Simpson's acquittal, 77% of white respondents thought that Simpson was guilty, and that the jury had made the wrong decision. African-American respondents saw the case very differently; only 29% thought that O.J. should have been convicted.[6] Studies of jury decision-making in capital cases have also shown that the race of the defendant and the racial composition of the jury have a significant impact on sentencing and whether the defendant receives the death penalty as opposed to life imprisonment (see Bowers, Steiner and Sandys, 2001).

Mock trial simulations have confirmed that race may affect juror decision-making in criminal cases involving black defendants and white victims. Bernard (1979) found differences between black and white jurors' verdicts in the hypothetical trial of a black defendant accused of assaulting a white police officer. Miller and Hewitt (1978) reported similar results and suggested that such differences may be a function of racial similarities between jurors and the victim. In their study, they found that 80% of black mock jurors favored conviction in a trial with a black victim, but that the percentage of black jurors voting to convict dropped to only 48% when the victim was white. Similarly, 65% of white jurors in the study voted for conviction when the victim was white, compared to only 32% of white jurors when the victim was black.[7]

Sommers and Ellsworth (2000) have also looked at the effects of race on criminal verdicts. They found that the racial identity of the defendant, on its own, was not enough to alter jurors' judgments of a case, and that any effects of the defendant's race depended on the salience of racial issues presented at trial. They ran an experiment in which groups of mock jurors were presented with summaries of a criminal trial against either a white or a black defendant. In one version of the summary, jurors read a passage designed to make race a very salient issue to the case. In the second, the description did not describe the case in openly racial terms. Sommers and Ellsworth hypothesized that making race more salient would raise white jurors' concerns about avoiding prejudice, and therefore reduce any effect of the defendant's race on white jurors' judgments of the case. Indeed, the white jurors who heard the "race salient" description were just as likely to find the black and white defendants guilty, whereas white jurors that read a "race neutral" description of the case were more likely to find the black defendant guilty than the white defendant. Black jurors were more lenient toward a black defendant in both of the experimental conditions, which Sommers and Ellsworth attribute to the constant salience of racial issues to black jurors.

In a different study, Sommers (2006) again observed a difference in white jurors' decision-making when they were exposed to race-salient information. Sommers presented groups of jurors with two different sets of voir dire questions. One set of questions asked jurors only general questions about the case and whether or not they could be fair. The second set included all of the items from the first, but also asked questions about race, the criminal justice system, and the juror's own attitudes toward black people. After both groups heard the same trial summary, Sommers found that only 34.4% of participants who were asked the voir dire questions about race voted to convict, compared to 47.1% of jurors who received the race-neutral questionnaire. Sommers theorized that the questions about race during voir dire "primed" white jurors to think about race and activated their concerns about violating norms of equality by appearing to be prejudiced.

A handful of studies have also identified links between jurors' race and their verdicts in civil trials. Looking at civil damages awards across the country, Helland and Tabarrok (2003) found significant correlations between the racial and socio-economic demographics of a trial venue and the size of civil damages awards from the courts in that venue. Specifically, they found that as the percentage of African-Americans in a county increased, so too did the average damages award in that venue. Specifically, a one percentage point increase in the proportion of African-Americans in a venue correlated with an increase in the average jury award in that county of $11,000. Similarly, a one percentage point increase in the proportion of Latinos living in a country corresponded to an increase of $17,000 in the average award. Helland and Tabarrok also found significant relationships between the poverty rate in a given county and the mean damages award from civil trials held there. A one percentage-point increase in the poverty rate in a county corresponded to an increase in the mean award of approximately $36,000. Race and poverty also had a combined effect on damages; Helland and Tabarrok found that a one percent increase in the black or Latino poverty rates in a county translated to an increase in the average damages award of 3-10% in civil trials in that county.

Hastie, Schkade and Payne (1998) also found correlations between demographics and verdicts in civil lawsuits. They showed short, videotaped synopses of four different civil cases to 726 mock jurors from the Denver, Colorado area. After viewing the videos and reading an additional information sheet about the case, jurors were asked to decide whether or not to award punitive damages to the plaintiff. Hastie *et al.* found a correlation between race and damages awards, with white jurors less likely than non-whites to award punitive damages. The researchers also found that jurors with higher incomes were less likely to award punitive damages.

Bornstein and Rajki (1994) also found that jurors' demographics influenced their judgments in a hypothetical civil lawsuit. In the experiment, 237 mock jurors from Baton Rouge, Louisiana read about a woman who claimed that a corporation's product caused her to develop ovarian cancer. Comparing jurors' verdicts across racial groups, Bornstein and Rajki found that 54% of minority jurors found the defendant liable, compared to only 39% of white jurors.

And in yet another study of jurors' reactions to several different civil lawsuits, Denove and Imwinkelreid found differences between white and black mock jurors' verdict preferences. The researchers recruited 400 mock jurors from the Sacramento and Los Angeles areas. The mock jurors read short descriptions of several different civil lawsuits. Denove and Imwinkelreid found that:

> Race emerges from the data as the single most important factor in predicting juror orientation. The impact of race is so strong that it often outweighs the impact of all other demographic factors

> combined. Specifically, African-American respondents were much more plaintiff-oriented than Caucasians on both liability and damages (Denove and Imwinkelreid, 1995, pg. 293).

In one case involving a woman who slipped and fell while walking into a grocery store on a rainy day, Denove and Imwinkelreid found that 72% of African-American jurors found for the plaintiff, compared to only 43% of white jurors.

Diamond, Saks and Landsmann (1999) looked for links between demographics and verdicts in a mock civil trial involving asbestos-related injuries. Using data from 1,042 mock jurors drawn from Cook County, Illinois, the researchers found that jurors' gender, race, education and income were all related to their verdicts in a model of juror decision making that included only jurors' demographics. However, once information about the case and jurors' attitudes were added to the model, only education and income remained statistically-significant demographic predictors of verdict.

In summary, while the bulk of the literature has concluded that juror race is usually irrelevant to the outcome of criminal and civil trials, several recent studies suggest that there may in fact be a relationship.

Linking Juror Gender and Verdicts

Several studies have investigated the effects of juror gender on verdicts, but the literature has yet to yield consistent conclusions. In her study on the effects of gender and jury behavior, Fowler reviews several studies that find gender differences in civil and criminal trials, but also reports that, "some research finds no support for the idea that males and females behave differently as jurors" (Fowler, 2005, pg. 25). For example, Hastie, Penrod and Pennington report that, "jurors who rendered verdicts on four different sets of trial materials... exhibited no gender differences," with the exception of rape trials, in which female jurors appeared to be somewhat more conviction prone than male jurors (Hastie, Penrod and Pennington, 1983, pg. 140). Hans and Vidmar arrived at a similar conclusion about the lack of consistent findings, arguing that, "in the majority of studies, there are no significant differences in the way men and women perceive and react to trials... a few studies find women more defense-oriented, while still others show women more favorable to the prosecutor" (Hans and Vidmar, 1986, pg. 76).

Research on the effects of juror gender on civil trial verdicts has also yielded inconsistent results. Some studies have found no effects of gender on verdicts. Green (1968), for example, found no gender differences in verdict preferences in a mock civil trial involving charges of negligence against the owner of a swimming pool. Nagel and Weitzman (1972) reported that gender had no effect on a juror's likelihood of finding for the plaintiff, but they did find that female jurors awarded larger damages on average than male jurors.

Denove and Imwinklereid found some gender effects, but reported that these effects depended on the type of case. From their mixed results, Denove and Imwinklereid concluded that, "it would be a mistake to classify either sex as strongly oriented for the plaintiff in the 'overall sense'" (Denove and Imwinkelreid, 1995, pg. 302). In her review of the literature on gender and civil jury verdicts, Bonazzoli confirms the uncertainty surrounding the effects of juror gender, reporting that, "the available findings indicate that the effect of juror gender on estimations of liability and the magnitude of damages awards is uncertain" (Bonazzoli, 1998, pg. 259).

Linking Juror Attitudes and Verdicts

Just as most studies of juror decision-making have concluded that race and gender are irrelevant to trial outcomes, most studies of jurors' attitudes have also failed to identify strong links between beliefs and verdicts. For example, Hastie, Penrod and Pennington point out that, "More than 160 jury studies provide little systematic evidence that personality variables, such as authoritarianism, locus of control, and legal attitudes, provide the predictive power needed to detect and challenge biased jurors" (Hastie, Penrod and Pennington, 1983, pg. 127). While attitudes may play a negligible role in jurors' judgments of criminal cases, some recent studies on civil trials have identified several attitudes that often correlate with jurors' verdict decisions.

Attitudes about Litigation and the Civil Justice System

Perhaps not surprisingly, one of the attitudes that may influence a juror's impression of a case is her beliefs about lawsuits and the state of the civil justice system. Boyll describes the extreme positions of this attitude:

> there appears to be an attitudinal set predisposed to feel that victims should always be compensated, regardless of fault. This idea is contrasted with 'tort reformers' who strongly hold that damage awards are excessive and must be curtailed (Boyll, 1991, pg. 179).

Polls and interviews suggest that a majority of Americans currently feel that there is a "litigation crisis" in the country, that most lawsuits are frivolous, and that damages awards tend to be excessive. Hans notes, "The mistrustful attitudes about civil litigation I uncovered [through post-trial juror interviews] are virtually identical to those found in national surveys" (Hans, 2000, pg. 217).

Whether such a "litigation crisis" actually exists is debatable, but jurors' beliefs about the civil justice system can affect their verdicts ((see Vidmar and Hans, 2007, pp. 274). Hans' found that, "attitudes about a litigation crisis were significantly associated with judgments in civil cases" (Hans, 2000, pg. 217). Diamond, Saks and Landsmann (1999) had similar results, finding that jurors who felt that plaintiffs generally win too much money from lawsuits were more likely to find for the defense.

Attitudes Toward Big Business

Corporate defendants frequently claim that they face an uphill battle for the hearts and minds of jurors, because jurors come to court with biases against big business. Whether such a disadvantage in fact exists is uncertain, as jurors may also come to court suspicious of the plaintiff's motives in bringing suit. But jurors' attitudes toward business corporations can affect their verdicts (see Vidmar and Hans, 2007, pp. 278-9). For example, Denove and Imwinkelreid found that mock jurors who agreed with the statement, "Manufacturers are willing to sell unsafe products" were more likely to find a defendant liable in four out of five hypothetical civil trials (Denove and Imwinkelried, 1995, pg. 326). Diamond, Saks and Landsmann (1999) reported similar results, finding that jurors who had generally positive attitudes toward big business were less likely to find for the plaintiff in a lawsuit against a large corporation. Conversely, jurors who thought that regulation of business was needed to ensure public welfare were more likely to find for the plaintiff.

Other studies have looked at the effect of the defendant's identity on jurors' perceptions of a civil case.

Hans and Ermann (1989) asked two groups of randomly-assigned mock jurors to decide a hypothetical civil lawsuit. The only difference in the evidence presented to the jurors was that one group heard that the defendant was a corporation ("The Jones Corporation") while the other group heard that the defendant was an individual ("Mr. Jones"). Hans and Ermann found that the group hearing about the fictional corporate defendant applied a higher standard of responsibility, judged the corporation to be more reckless and morally wrong and, as a result, awarded higher damages than the group that heard about the individual defendant.

Denove and Imwinkelreid (1995) ran a similar experiment. Their hypothetical case involved a woman who became ill after eating an improperly-cooked hamburger. Half of the subjects heard that the defendant was a large restaurant chain, while the other half heard that the defendant was an individual.[8] Jurors in both groups were asked what amount of money, if any, they would award to compensate the plaintiff for her injuries. Of those jurors who heard that the defendant was a business, 80% thought the defendant should pay some compensatory damages. In the group that heard that the defendant was an individual, only 39% thought that the defendant should pay. The median damages award also differed between the two groups; jurors in the "business defendant" group averaged $14,000, compared to a median of only $4,100 in the group that heard that the defendant was an individual (Denove and Imwinkelreid, 1995, pg. 330-2).

Jurors' Political Ideology

Political ideology is another individual-level factor that could conceivably affect jurors' decision-making. While relatively few studies examine its role in jury verdicts, the research concluded that jurors' politics make little or no difference to their verdicts. For example, in their study of 800 mock jurors, Hastie, Penrod and Pennington found that, "the jury's final verdict [was] unrelated to ideological orientation" (Hastie, Penrod and Pennington, 1983, pg. 140). Denove and Imwinkelreid also failed to find any links between political ideology and verdict, reporting that, "political orientation had minimal impact" on jurors verdicts in four different mock trials (Denove and Imwinkelreid, 1995, pg. 325).

DATA ON CIVIL JUROR DECISION-MAKING

The discussion this far has revealed that most scholars have found little or no relationship between juror's demographics and their verdicts. However, one must remember that there are two possible explanations for such "non-findings." The first is that researchers have reliable data, have used the best available research methods and have reached a convincing finding about the lack of any relationship between the subjects being studied. The second possibility is that such "non-findings" are the result of some problem with the research, such as unreliable or missing data. In other words, an absence of proof is not necessarily proof of absence. Relationships may exist between juror characteristics and verdicts, but shortcomings in the studies have prevented researchers from fully appreciating those relationships.

One common problem throughout the empirical literature on jury decision-making is a lack of reliable data. Data on juror decision-making, particularly in civil lawsuits, is extremely scarce. With very few exceptions, legal restrictions limit researchers' access to jurors during trials.[9] In fact, researchers who tried to use data from real jury trials in the past faced severe consequences. For example, in the 1950s:

> as part of a large study of trial by jury, researchers obtained the permission of the judge and counsel and tape-recorded the jury deliberations in five Kansas civil cases. Even though the recordings were made only for research purposes, when the fact of the tapings became known to the public, there was a huge outcry. The taping was censured by the United States Attorney General and the researchers had to appear before the Subcommittee on Internal Security of the Senate Judiciary Committee. Over thirty jurisdictions then passed laws specifically forbidding the recording of jury deliberations (Hans and Vidmar, 1986, pg. 99).

As a result of restrictions on researchers' access to juries during their deliberations, studies of juror decision-making typically make use of one of three alternative sources of data, including 1) data from interviews conducted with jurors after the trial has ended, 2) data on the verdicts of mock jurors who participate in simulated trials, and 3) archival data on verdicts and awards collected at the level of the trial venue. Each of these data sources has advantages and disadvantages relative to the others for understanding juror behavior.

Post-Trial Juror Interviews

Interviews with jurors conducted after their service has ended allow researchers to talk to "real" jurors, as opposed to individuals who participate in trial simulations. However, data drawn from post-trial juror interviews suffer from several problems. Jurors' memories of the details of a case can fade quickly and jurors' recollections of the trial may be distorted by the deliberation process.[10] For example, jurors may be unwilling to admit that they were in the minority during deliberations, or that they disagreed at some point with the eventual verdict. Sommers and Ellsworth point out that juror interviews, "rely entirely on jurors' self-reported perceptions and their memory of the experiences. It is a well-documented psychological findings that people frequently lack the ability to identify accurately the factors that influence their judgment and behavior" (Sommers and Ellsworth, 2003, pg. 1000). Post-trial interviews are also time-consuming and expensive and as a result, sample sizes in studies that rely on interviews tend to be small. In order to build a data set large enough for reliable statistical analysis, the researcher must also interview jurors from several different trials, meaning that jurors have heard different information presented by different attorneys.[11] Because the jurors have heard different cases, it is difficult to separate the effects of the evidence from any other influences on jurors' verdict decisions.

Mock Trials

The most common source of data on juror decision-making is trial simulations or "mock trials." Mock trials involve the recruitment of "mock jurors"—often college students but ideally jury-eligible individuals drawn from the community at large—who are asked to render a verdict or give their reactions to a condensed version of a trial. Mock trials allow for a great deal of control over both the evidence presented and the numerous other aspects of a trial that may affect jurors' views of a case. This control is a clear advantage of trial simulations over field studies of actual jurors' verdicts, where no such control is possible.

However, conducting mock trial research is expensive. Just the costs of recruiting mock jurors can be prohibitive.

Because of the expense involved, researchers must often take short-cuts when recruiting their samples. Sample sizes in such studies are often modest,[12] and many studies make use of "convenience samples" recruited by approaching potential research participants in malls, grocery stores and other crowded areas.[13] Such samples are not randomly-selected and are therefore often not representative of the communities from which they are drawn. The use of unrepresentative samples of mock jurors raises questions about the external validity of the research findings.

An alternative to the expensive recruitment of mock jurors from the community is the use of college students as research subjects. By one estimate, more than two-thirds of the published studies on mock trials use students as jurors (Bray and Kerr, 1982, pg. 293). While students are relatively inexpensive experimental subjects and are readily available to university researchers, students are often not ideal research subjects. Students' attitudes and decision-making processes may differ in important ways from those of adults in the general population. For example, Bray and Kerr point out that, in terms of social science experiments, "there is little doubt that college students often behave differently from the adult population" (Bray and Kerr, 1982, pg. 310). Studies have demonstrated that students differed from "real" people in both their reactions to trial testimony and their verdicts (see Howard and Leber, 1988, and Field and Barnett, 1978). Sears (1985) has argued that social psychology's over-reliance on college students as experimental subjects may have even given researchers a biased view of human nature. Because of these concerns, Devine, *et al.* stated that:

> In the future, to improve generalizability, it would be preferable to use randomly selected individuals from jury pool lists as opposed to college students,

who are not representative of the typical jury pool (Devine, *et al.*, 2001, pg. 709).

Another problem with the use of students in studies of juror decision-making, particularly in studies on the effects of demographics and other individual-level factors, is the fact that college student samples offer much less variance in many demographic categories than would a sample of subjects drawn randomly from the community at large. College students are almost all the same age and, by definition, have the same level of education. Student samples are also more likely to over-represent higher socio-economic groups.

Yet another concern about mock trials research is the quality of the evidence presented to the mock jurors and the realism of the courtroom experience. Many trial simulations offer jurors nothing more than short, written descriptions of a lawsuit. For example, the "trial" in Bornstein and Rajki's 1994 research was a one-page written description of the case that participants read at a table set up next to a department store. The lack of realism in most trial simulations raises questions about the ecological validity of any findings from that research. If the mock trial simulation is unlike the experience of a real trial, one can not conclude that the factors that influence behavior in the simulation will also affect juror behavior in the courtroom.[14] Citing the numerous studies that use "brief, non-detailed case materials," Bray and Kerr point out that, "the artificiality of most laboratory experiments and experimental simulations has led many observers to argue that the findings of this literature are of limited or no value in describing actual behavior in the courtroom" (Bray and Kerr, 1982, pg. 305). Weiten and Diamond make a similar argument: "insofar as future researchers are interested in the generalizability of their findings, they should procure more representative samples [and] employ more realistic trial simulations, such as lengthy and complex audio and videotaped trials" (Weiten and Diamond, 1979, pg. 83).

Critics of mock trial methodology also point out that participants know that their verdicts will not have any real-world consequences. Indeed, most studies of mock jurors simply ask the participants to behave "as if" they were real jurors hearing a real case. However, the jurors know that no one will go to jail (or worse) or face a large damages award as a result of their mock verdicts. As a result, mock jurors may not take the research seriously or give their decision as much consideration as they would, were they in a real court of law.[15] One way to mitigate this problem is to engage the research subjects in "active role playing" in which participants render verdicts, award damages and deliberate with one another to reach a verdict. In such active, realistic trial simulations, jurors take their decisions very seriously. They become emotionally involved in their verdicts, and often argue passionately with other jurors during deliberations, as if the trial were real.[16] Having viewed many mock trial deliberations, Priest notes:

> Even in the experimental setting, [jurors] work hard, attempt to do their best, interact well with one another, and almost never engage in selfish or strategic behavior… no observer could fail to be impressed with the seriousness, decency, and common sense with which jurors from diverse walks of life approach their task (Priest, 2002, p. vii).

In short, mock trial simulations offer researchers a great deal of control over the evidence presented and other variables of potential interest. However, the expense of such research often forces researchers to take short-cuts in terms of the quality of the sample of mock jurors. For the same financial reasons, mock trials may also fail to simulate accurately the trial experience, with evidence presented in a form very different from what jurors would see and hear at a real trial. These problems have raised serious questions about the validity of the findings of such research.

Archival Verdict Data

A third source of data on civil juror decision-making is archival information on actual verdicts rendered across the country. These data sets include information at the level of the trial, such as the jury's verdict, any damages awarded, the location of the trial and perhaps some information about the type of case. When combined with census data on the demographics of the trial venue, researchers can look for correlations between the verdicts and awards in an area and that area's population characteristics. These data have the strong advantage of reflecting actual trial verdicts. Many of these data sets also include many thousands of observations, allowing researchers to perform sophisticated statistical analyses.

Several organizations keep track of data on civil trial verdicts. The Administrative Office of the United States Courts keeps track of verdicts from all federal civil lawsuits. However, the only information recorded in the database for each trial is the verdict, any award, and the general type of case. Nothing is recorded about the litigants, the evidence, the attorneys, the judge or any of the other factors that could conceivably affect the outcome of the trial. Another shortcoming of the data on federal civil verdicts is that damages are "top-coded." This means that the highest damages award recorded in the data is $9,999,000, even if the actual award is much higher. This may result in a significant under-reporting of the size of actual awards. A second source of data is the Civil Trial Court Network, which records verdicts from civil trials in state courts. The information recorded is similar to that in the federal court data base, in that it is limited to the verdict and general type of case for each trial. However, the state court data includes records for only 45 counties across the country.[17] The 45 counties represented in the database are selected from among the country's 75 most populous counties, and are therefore not a random or representative sample of all trial venues. A third source of archival data on jury verdicts is Jury Verdicts Research (JVR) whose data base contains information on 122,444 trials, settlements and arbitrations conducted from 1988 to 1997. The JVR data contain the same information as the state and federal data bases mentioned above, but also include additional information on the injuries claimed by the plaintiff. However, JVR's data collection strategy focuses on "precedent setting awards" in civil lawsuits. The focus on these large awards means that JVR data are biased toward the high end of jury awards.[18]

Studies that use archival trial data also rely on census data to look for correlations between jury verdicts and demographic variables. The use of census data assumes that the demographics of the trial venue (a county in state courts and several counties in a federal court district) are identical, or at least similar to, those of the jury pool. However, this may not be the case. While the sources of the lists from which potential jurors' names are drawn has expanded considerably in recent decades to include voters, drivers, and even telephone customers, there is still evidence of the systematic under-representation of some groups on juries (See Van Dyke, 1977). Another concern with the use of census data on demographics is that large urban counties may have multiple courthouses. Different courthouses in the same county may draw jurors from different communities, which often differ considerably from one another in terms of their demographic compositions. As a result, courts within the same county may empanel juries with very different demographic make-ups, meaning that the census data for the county as a whole will not accurately reflect the composition of the juries seated at a particular county courthouse. Finally, these archival data do not allow for any analysis of the effects on verdicts of some demographic variables, such as gender and age, as these factors do not vary appreciably across trial venues.

While the sample sizes in these archival data sets are larger than those typically seen in studies using juror interviews or trial simulations, a major drawback of such data is the lack of any control over the types of cases heard or the evidence presented. There is no way to know about the exact types of cases going to trial, the strength of the competing evidence in those trials or the competence of the presenting attorneys. This comparison of apples and oranges means that one can not be sure of the extent to which jurors' demographics may have affected their verdicts. Saks summarizes the problems with archival data:

> Archival studies showing that certain jurors in certain places found for plaintiffs some percentage of the time, or awarded some mean or median (or other) amount of damages, might seem at first blush to allow the inference that jurors of one kind are more prone to finding for the plaintiffs than jurors of another kind, or that jurors of one region are more tight-fisted than jurors of another region. But without more, those studies can not support such an inference because the data are likely to be confounded by differences between trial units:

> different law, different circumstances giving rise to the case facts, different industries, different sub-cultures, systematically different sets of facts, different quality of fact presentation, different costs of injuries, and so on... In short, the mix of cases going to the juries likely differs from place to place, and possibly quite a bit, so that what seems like greater generosity among jurors may actually be a response to injuries or costs that differ in magnitude. Unless an effort is made to measure (and, if necessary, to statistically hold constant) the mix of cases going to the jury, it is impossible to meaningfully compare what different juries in different places do with the cases given to them (Saks, 2002, pg. 1882-3).

In short, because these data sets include only the most general information about each trial—typically just a broad classification, such as "medical malpractice" or "product liability"—little or no control is possible over the variations in evidence presented in each case.

Weighing the Strengths and Weaknesses of Different Data Sources

The three types of data typically seen in the literature on juror decision-making offer researchers a trade-off. Post-trial juror interviews allow researchers access to real jurors, but for any meaningful statistical analysis, researchers must interview jurors from many different trials. The use of jurors from different trials does not allow for control over the evidence the jurors hear. Data collection through interviews is also expensive and time-consuming, resulting in rather small sample sizes. Mock trials allow for controls on the evidence presented, but the costs involved restrict the sample size or necessitate the use of "convenience samples" or college students as research subjects. Mock trials with limited evidence and questionable realism also raise concerns about the ecological and external validity of the research. Finally, data taken from actual jury verdicts at the level of the trial venue offer the opportunity to study large samples of actual jury verdicts. However, there is no control for the types of cases heard or the evidence presented, and there may be significant differences between the demographic information drawn from census records and the actual composition of the juries in the venue.[19]

In a perfect world, jury researchers would have access to a data set that contained information on the individual verdict decisions of several thousand real jurors, who all happened to hear the same case. Of course, no such data exist. The next best source of data would be realistically-conducted mock trials, with controls over the evidence presented, involving a large sample of mock jurors drawn to match the demographics of their respective jury pools. But such data are extremely rare, and this scarcity of reliable data may have led researchers to some incorrect conclusions about the relationship between jurors' characteristics and their verdict decisions.

Statistical Methods in the Jury Decision-Making Literature

Concerns about methodology in jury decision-making studies do not stop with the quality of the data. The statistical methods used to analyze the data in many studies of juror decision-making are less than ideal and may have given researchers only a partial picture of the relationship between jurors' characteristics and their verdicts.

Many studies of juror decision-making use rather rudimentary statistical methods that are not the best tool for analyzing the data. For example, in their frequently cited study, Denove and Imwinkelreid (1995) simply compare verdict percentages between different groups of jurors, without any evaluation of statistical significance. Other studies rely solely on simple bivariate correlations or cross-tabulations that measure correlations between verdict decisions and individual demographic categories.[20] These studies report small correlations or statistically-insignificant cross-tabulations, and from that evidence argue that jurors' demographics have no bearing on their verdicts. But many demographic categories are correlated with one another. For example, education and income tend to be highly correlated; the more education a person has, the more that person tends to earn. Looking at only one demographic variable at a time can mask or distort the "true" relationship between variables. A multivariate model, in which the potentially confounding effects of demographics are controlled, can more accurately estimate the importance of jurors' characteristics on their verdict decisions.

Many studies also rely on a "goodness of fit" statistical measure, such as the R-squared statistic, to evaluate the importance of demographic factors on jurors' verdicts. Such "goodness of fit" statistics measure the amount of variation in the dependent variable (in most cases, jurors' verdicts) accounted for by variation in the independent variables (the jurors' characteristics). In other words, the R-squared statistic measures how well demographic variables "explain" the observed differences in jurors' verdicts. Many studies of juror decision-making report rather low R-squared statistics—often less than 10%—in models using juror characteristics to predict verdicts. From these results, researchers have argued that demographics have little or no relevance to jurors' verdict decisions.[21]

However, one must approach these "goodness of fit" measures with a bit of caution. The goal of statistical models of juror decision-making is not to "explain" or "account for" all of the variation in jurors' verdicts. While many fields of research (typically those in the natural sciences) may seek to formulate perfect predictive models with R-squared statistics approaching 100%, researchers in the social sciences can only dream of such precision. Students of juror behavior—and human behavior in general—must recognize that there are many hundreds of variables that may affect a person's actions, and that precise prediction of any human behavior with a relatively small number of explanatory variables is impossible. The goal of empirical research on jurors' decision-making is not to account for all of the possible factors that might affect a juror's verdict. Instead, the goal is to test whether variables of interest, such as jurors' background characteristics and attitudes, have a statistically- and substantively-significant relationship with their verdicts. Rather than relying exclusively on the R-squared statistic or some similar measure, a better approach to the problem would be to evaluate the substantive and statistical effects of the explanatory variables on verdict decisions.

Differentiating the Criminal and the Civil Jury

The consensus in the literature that jurors' characteristics have little to do with their verdicts is a product of studies that focus disproportionately on the criminal jury. Civil juries have received far less attention. Rose and Vidmar noted that, "Although the complicated relationship between race and criminal jury verdicts has been and remains an active area of social science research, the effect of demographic characteristics on civil jury verdicts has received far less scholarly attention" (Rose and Vidmar, 2002, pg. 1889-90). The disproportionate interest in criminal verdicts is understandable, as verdicts in criminal trials are seen as weightier and more important than those in civil cases.[22] If convicted, criminal defendants face lengthy imprisonment or even death. Verdicts in civil lawsuits, in contrast, involve "only" monetary awards. While civil damages awards may be very large and gain national media attention, the criminal verdict consistently dominates popular and academic interest in the workings of the jury.

Often lost in the relatively few studies on civil juries is the fact that criminal and civil cases make very different demands on the jurors that hear them. Specifically, the decision facing a civil jury is quite different from that of its criminal counterpart, and as a result, conclusions drawn about what motivates jurors' decisions in criminal cases can not necessarily be extrapolated to jurors' decisions in civil cases. The nature of the civil verdict decision, discussed in greater detail below, may allow jurors' attitudes and characteristics to play a larger role in the verdict decision than they would in a criminal case. As a result, while jurors' demographics may have little to do with their verdicts in most criminal trials, one can not necessarily extrapolate from that finding that demographics are irrelevant in civil trials.

The nature of the tort claims that most often draw attention to the civil justice system center on questions of negligence. When deciding questions of negligence, jurors are instructed to evaluate the defendant's actions in relation to those of an "ordinary" or "reasonable" person in a similar situation. The importance of the term "ordinary" is evident in the definition of negligence given to jurors in a recent product liability trial in Texas:

> Negligence means failure to use ordinary care; that is to say, failure to do that which a person of ordinary prudence would have done under the same or similar circumstances, or not doing that which a person of ordinary prudence would not have done, under the same or similar circumstances.

Similarly, a defective product must be "unreasonably dangerous," which is often defined as a product that "is more dangerous than would be contemplated by the ordinary user with ordinary knowledge." While the precise definitions of "defect" and "negligence" may vary from state to state, this language is typical.

Jonakait describes the question of negligence as requiring much more from the jury than a simple determination of fact. He writes:

> the verdict requires more than a mere resolution of what happened. It also requires a qualitative assessment of the reasonableness of the conduct. The jury in essence must define the appropriate standard of care for a given situation (Jonakait, 2003, pg. 65).

Indeed, what may be "reasonable" or "ordinary" to one person may not be to another. Although the decision of what is and is not ordinary and reasonable is highly subjective, Vidmar and Hans (2007) argue that the jury is uniquely qualified to apply the "reasonable person" standard, particularly compared to judges. Judges are members of a socio-economic elite, whereas juries are drawn from the community at large and may therefore better represent the values of that community.

Contrast the decision on negligence with the task facing the criminal jury. In criminal cases, jurors are asked to make a finding of fact about what happened, just as they are in civil trials. Jurors must determine whether or not the evidence presented proves beyond a reasonable doubt that the defendant committed an illegal act. Jurors must also consider some factors that may be open to interpretation, such as the defendant's intent. However, criminal cases assume that the alleged conduct was neither reasonable nor ordinary. Jurors are not required to evaluate the nature of the defendant's conduct to the same extent as they are in civil trials.

Viewed from the perspective of the decision-making task, one can see a potential explanation for the failure of the literature to appreciate the relationships between jurors' characteristics and their verdicts in civil cases. The literature focuses predominately on criminal trials, in which the juror's decision is less open to individual interpretation than is the verdict decision facing jurors in civil trials. While there is certainly room for jurors' interpretation in criminal cases, criminal juries are charged with evaluating the difference between the defendant's actions and the specific constraints of the criminal code. Jurors in civil trials, by contrast, must decide whether the evidence shows that the defendant failed to act in a reasonable or ordinary manner. This inherent subjectivity in the civil verdict decision opens the door for jurors' personal views to play a much greater role than they might in a criminal trial.

Thus, the disproportionate attention paid to decision-making by juries in criminal cases, combined with a failure to appreciate the very different tasks performed by the civil jury, as opposed to the criminal jury, may have also contributed to the questionable consensus in the literature that jurors' characteristics have no effect on their verdict decisions. While these findings may apply to most criminal trials, it may not be applicable to civil trials.

JURY RESEARCH AND THE COLOR BLIND IDEAL

The previous sections discussed methodological problems in much of the juror decision-making literature that may have prevented researchers from fully appreciating the role of individual-level factors in jurors' verdicts. At this point, another possible explanation for the consensus in the literature should be discussed. Put bluntly, researchers may not want to find a relationship between verdicts and such factors as race and gender, and may therefore have an incentive to overlook evidence of such relationships.

Early studies of juror decision-making paid little attention to questions of race and gender. Most studies focused on other areas, such as the effects of evidence and trial procedure, and treated juror-level factors as an after-thought. Sommers and Ellsworth point out that the early studies that formed the foundation for the consensus that race was irrelevant in jury verdicts focused on other areas of jury behavior:

> For many years, the consensus among mock jury researchers was that little if any consistent correlation existed between jurors' race and verdict preference. But the studies upon which this conclusion was based were not likely to reveal between-race differences in jurors decision-making. They were, for the most part, intended as investigations of nonracial issues such as evidence comprehension, case complexity, jury size, and jury instructions, and most had too few non-White jurors to permit valid statistical comparisons. In fact, participant race was often assessed for demographic

> purposes only, and null results for race were usually reported as peripheral findings (Sommers and Ellsworth, 2003, pg. 1017).

Thus the null results from these control variables formed the foundation of the early consensus that race had little impact on jury verdicts.

More recent studies have focused squarely on the effects of juror factors. While some of these studies reveal significant findings, many of them seem to go out of their way to down-play these results. In a 2002 article, for example, Eisenberg and Wells found relationships between race and verdict in several areas of civil litigation. They reported that in federal courts located in urban areas, "increasing black population percentages do correlate significantly with greater plaintiff win rates in all three cases categories [job discrimination, products and torts]" (Eisenberg and Wells, 2002, pg. 1861). Then, shortly after reporting these findings, they conclude that, "We find little robust evidence that a trial locale's population demographics help explain jury trial outcomes. In tort cases, jury trial awards and plaintiff success rates do not consistently increase significantly with black population percentage" (Eisenberg and Wells, 2002, pg. 1869).

Diamond, Saks and Landsmann, who are among the most prolific writers on juror decision-making, have also found correlations between demographic variables and verdicts.[23] In a mock civil suit involving claims of workplace asbestos exposure and illness, Diamond, Saks and Landsmann report that women were more likely to find for the plaintiff than men (55% vs. 47%), minorities were more plaintiff-oriented than were whites (63% vs. 46%) and jurors with only a high school education were more likely to find for the plaintiff (59%) than were jurors with a college degree (42%). These results were statistically significant in not only bivariate correlations, but also when combined into a multivariate model of juror decision-making (Diamond, Saks and Landsmann, 1999, pg. 306).

But rather than concede that demographics might matter to a juror's verdict preference, Diamond *et al.* dismiss these findings. They describe the significance of the demographic variables as a kind of unwanted by-product of their large sample size:

> In the present case we found that five of the ten background characteristics were significantly related to the juror's liability verdict preference. Although some of the relationships are weak, they emerge as statistically significant because the sample size (1,021) is substantial (Diamond, Saks and Landsmann, 1999, pg. 306).

They then point out that only 5.4% of the variation in verdicts was explained by demographic variables. Focusing on this single statistic and overlooking the substantial differences between jurors from different demographic backgrounds, Diamond, Saks and Landsmann conclude that, "background characteristics show only a modest association with verdict preferences" (Diamond, Saks and Landsmann, 1999, pg. 306).

In another study, Wissler, Hart and Saks looked at the relationship between jurors' damages awards and the severity of plaintiffs' injuries in a variety of hypothetical lawsuits. Wissler *et al.* also arrive at the conclusion that juror demographics are irrelevant to their verdict decisions, even after reporting statistically- and substantively-significant relationships between the size of damages awards and jurors' income and gender. They observed that:

> Of the sociodemographic characteristics, gender was the most strongly related to awards...Male

> jurors gave larger awards than female jurors, and jurors with higher household incomes gave larger awards than those with lower incomes (Wissler, Hart and Saks, 2000, pg. 783).

After reporting these findings, the Wissler *et al.* study ends with a surprising conclusion: "The present study, along with other recent research, suggests that what has been learned about liability verdicts can be extended to damages-relevant responses: individual differences make little difference" (Wissler, Hart and Saks, 2000, pg. 805).

Of the few researchers who have reported significant relationships between juror race and verdict, some seem to recant their findings in later research. One of the few articles to report significant relationships between jurors' demographics and their verdicts is Bornstein and Rajki's 1994 study of decision-making by mock civil jurors. In that study, 54% of minority jurors found the defendant liable, compared to only 39% of white jurors (Bornstein and Rajki, 1994). However, in a later work, Bornstein inexplicably reverses his earlier judgment. Bornstein's 2003 book on juror decision-making in civil lawsuits includes a chapter on the effects of juror-level variables on verdicts. He reviews the literature on the effects of jurors' characteristics, but for some reason fails to include his own article in that review. His review includes sections on the effects of juror economic status, political orientation, education and gender, but omits any discussion of the effects of juror race. His review concludes that, "demographic factors typically exert a weak and inconsistent influence on civil cases" (Greene and Bornstein, 2003).

Why would researchers want to overlook or downplay the evidence that jurors from different racial backgrounds might see trials differently and return different verdicts?

First of all, identifying differences between blacks and whites, or men and women, is controversial. Such claims can prompt charges of racism or sexism, and can seem to violate the egalitarian norms most Americans embrace. The days in which people believed that certain racial or ethnic groups were superior to others are behind us. Overwhelming majorities of Americans now claim to believe that all people are truly created equal and that everyone, regardless of race or gender, should have the same opportunities to exercise their faculties and pursue their ambitions. Yet despite the social advances of recent decades, race and gender continue to be sensitive and controversial topics, and a wish to avoid controversy may dissuade researchers from fully exploring the effects of juror-level variables.

Contributing to fears of controversy is the fact that the jury itself is intimately connected to issues of racial and gender discrimination. Until recently, women in some states were excluded from jury service because they were thought to lack the character or intellect needed to make difficult verdict decisions. It was also thought that being exposed to the gritty evidence of violent crimes could somehow damage women's fragile psyches (see, for example, *Hoyt v. Florida*, 1961). Identifying differences in verdict preferences between blacks and whites, or between men and women, can conjure up the old justifications for excluding large segments of the population from jury service.

Such concerns are certainly evident in Supreme Court rulings on the right to serve on juries. The Court clearly equates any claims of gender or racial difference with historic rationales used to exclude African-Americans and women from civic life:

> Exclusion of blacks from a jury, solely because of race, can be no more justified by a belief that blacks are less likely than whites to consider fairly or sympathetically the State's case against a black defendant than it can be justified by the notion that blacks lack the 'intelligence, experience, or moral integrity' (*Neal v. Delaware* 103 US 371 (1881)) to be entrusted with that role (*Batson v. Kentucky*, 1986, pg. 105, Justice Marshall, concurring).

The Court made a similar argument in 1994 about the exclusion of women from jury service:

> Respondent offers virtually no support for the conclusion that gender alone is an accurate predictor or jurors' attitudes; yet it urges this Court to condone the same stereotypes that justified the wholesale exclusion of women from juries and the ballot box (*J.E.B. v. Alabama*, 1994, pg. 138).

Thus, our country's long history of discrimination against women and ethnic minorities, and particularly in relation to jury service, makes claims of verdict differences based on race and gender problematic. Combine this concern with our strong egalitarian ethos, and the result may be to discourage researchers from focusing on such differences. Researchers may have a strong interest in overlooking, or at least downplaying, any relationship between individual-level variables and juror verdict preferences.

CONCLUSION

Studies on juror decision-making have repeatedly concluded that jurors' individual characteristics, particularly race and gender, have little or no effect on verdict outcomes. This chapter has argued that several common methodological problems in the literature have kept researchers from fully appreciating the importance of jurors' demographics on trial outcomes. Paramount among these methodological problems is a lack of reliable data on juror decision-making, particularly in civil trials. The next chapter will look at new data on jurors' verdicts to see if there might indeed be significant relationships between juror factors and verdicts in civil lawsuits.

CHAPTER 2:

Re-Examining the Link between Juror Factors and Verdicts

In the previous chapter, we saw that most of the scholarship on juror decision-making has concluded that little if any relationship exists between jurors' characteristics and their verdicts. This chapter will challenge that consensus. Through the analysis of new data in three different types of civil litigation, this chapter will argue that the characteristics of the members of a jury, including the jurors' race, gender, education, income and attitudes toward case-relevant issues, can have a strong influence on the verdict.[24]

THE DATA

To test the findings in the literature that jurors' traits have little or no effect on their verdicts, I collected data on juror decision-making in three different types of civil litigation. The data for this study are drawn from the archives of the firm of Mattson & Sherrod, Inc. Mattson & Sherrod, Inc. is a Los Angeles-based litigation consulting firm that develops trial strategies and jury-selection criteria for Fortune 500 clients facing major civil litigation. To this end, Mattson & Sherrod, Inc. organizes, runs and analyzes mock trials in venues across the United States.

Each mock trial takes place in the venue where the real trial will be held. Mattson & Sherrod, Inc. contracts with a market research firm in the trial venue to recruit a sample of mock jurors that reflects the demographic characteristics of the local jury pool. Prospective mock jurors are contacted by telephone using a combination of random digit dialing and phone number data bases. Mock jurors must meet all of the requirements for jury service in the trial venue. Mock trials are held in hotel meeting rooms or conference centers and participants in the mock trial are paid for their time.

Before hearing any evidence, the mock jurors complete an extensive battery of questions about themselves. This questionnaire includes standard demographic questions, as well as numerous multiple-choice questions concerning jurors' attitudes toward government and politics, lawsuits, business corporations, economic regulation and other topics.

After completing the initial questionnaire, jurors see a condensed version of each side's case presented by real attorneys, either live or on videotape.[25] The duration of the presentations range from one-hour videotaped summaries of each side's case, to extended three-day sessions that feature live presentations of opening statements, cases-in-chief and closing arguments. In all of the mock trials, jurors see the actual evidence from the case, including important documents and excerpts from witness depositions. After the conclusion of both sides' presentations, each juror completes a questionnaire about their reactions to the case that includes a question about which side the juror thinks should win the case.

For this study, data from mock trials conducted in numerous locations across the country between 1996 and 2005 have been aggregated into three data sets, each involving a different type of civil litigation. The first data set was assembled from eight mock trials conducted for a major auto manufacturer. In these eight cases, plaintiffs brought suit against the automaker after a serious vehicle accident. Plaintiffs alleged that the accidents and resulting injuries were the result of design defects in the vehicle. In its defense, the manufacturer claimed that its vehicle was adequately tested, had no design defects and that the accidents and resulting injuries were caused by driver error.

The second data set includes information drawn from nine mock trials held for the manufacturer of a prescription medication. Plaintiffs in these cases alleged that the medication carried severe and even life-threatening side-effects which the manufacturer failed to disclose to doctors or patients. In its defense, the drug manufacturer claimed that its drug was safe and effective, that epidemiological studies revealed no links between its medication and serious side-effects, and that any illnesses experienced by patients were the result of either patient abuse of the medication or pre-existing medical conditions.

The third data set is the product of seventeen mock trials held on behalf of a large accounting firm. The plaintiffs in these cases were corporations that alleged that errors and oversights by the accounting firm caused them to suffer financial losses and that the accounting firm should therefore compensate the company for those damages. In its defense, the accounting firm argued that its work was of a high quality, that its accountants and auditors were well-trained and highly-qualified, and that the company adhered to all relevant professional standards of conduct. The defendant argued that the losses were the result of poor business decisions made by the client company, rather than any actions by the accounting firm. (For more information on the trial venues, the demographic make-up of the mock juries and the sample sizes, see Appendix A.)

The data in this study avoid many of the methodological problems common in the jury decision-making literature. The mock jurors in these studies are all drawn from the community at large (as opposed to college students, who serve as jurors in many mock jury studies) and are recruited to be representative samples of the local jury pool. The data span numerous venues across the country, as opposed to a single area, while controlling for most of the variance in the evidence presented. That is, jurors heard cases that are almost identical in terms of the case issues involved. Real litigators present the evidence in a realistic trial setting and a great deal of trial evidence is presented, in contrast to studies that rely on short videos or brief written descriptions of a case as the trial "evidence." The use of a representative sample of "real" people recruited from the trial venue, combined with real attorneys and realistic courtroom conditions, increases confidence in the validity of the conclusions drawn from an analysis of the data.

While these data are superior in many ways to most of what appears in the literature, there are some limitations. Like any mock trial study, jurors in these situations are not rendering a real verdict. In a major civil trial, jurors must grapple with the weighty decisions of whether or not to award millions (or even billions) of dollars. In a mock trial, the verdicts carry no such real-world consequences. However, people do become very involved in mock trial simulations, and they behave much as they would if they were real jurors. Mock jurors take their decisions very seriously, and it is not uncommon for deliberating mock jurors to make impassioned arguments, shout, pound on the table, and become highly emotional while debating the case. Krupat points out that the active participation of research subjects in a realistic simulation puts the subjects in the same frame of mind they would have in the actual situation. He writes, "In active role playing subjects do not sit passively and predict what they might do in a situation…Rather they actively participate, they 'go to the moon'" (Krupat, 1977, pg. 501).

There are several other differences between the experiences of mock jurors and those of real jurors. Real jurors undergo voir dire, during which they may be required to answer questions posed by the court or the attorneys about their attitudes toward issues relevant to the case. Mock jurors undergo no such scrutiny. However, mock jurors are screened during the recruiting process, and employees of the companies involved in the lawsuit, as well as their immediate family members, are not allowed to participate. Mock jurors also hear a brief introduction to the case. After this introduction, jurors are asked whether they can be fair and impartial. Jurors will occasionally report that they have reason to doubt their impartiality. These jurors are questioned further in private, and if there is cause to doubt their impartiality, they are excused from the exercise.

It should also be noted that the individual mock trials that make up the three data sets do not include exactly the same evidence. While the car accident cases all involve the same make and model of vehicle and the same defect allegations, other factors, such as the particular details of the accident and the severity of the injuries, necessarily vary somewhat from case to case. Similarly, while all of the prescription drug cases involve the same medication, the injuries claimed by the users of the drug vary somewhat in terms of severity, as do the length of time the patients used the drug, and the patients' pre-existing medical conditions.

Finally, in the accounting malpractice cases, the allegations vary somewhat, and include charges of incorrect audits, bad tax advice and flawed business strategies. However, the general allegations of professional misconduct, malpractice and negligence are similar from case to case. Also, in all three areas of litigation, the damages requested by the plaintiffs vary from case to case. However, the major case themes within each of the three data sets are the same, as are the identities of the defendants and the plaintiffs' main allegations. Moreover, as will be seen in the following sections, the models of juror decision-making account for these minor variations in the evidence.

PRELIMINARY DATA ANALYSIS

An initial comparison of jurors' verdicts by race and gender reveals significant differences between white and black jurors, and between men and women, in each of the three areas of civil litigation. Consider first the car accident cases. A simple cross-tabulation of verdict by juror race shows that 66% of black jurors found for the plaintiff, compared to only 30.5% of white jurors. These differences are also statistically significant ($X^2<0.000$). Black jurors voted for the plaintiff at a higher rate than white jurors in all but two of the venues. The two exceptions were the Libby, Montana trial, where the jury included only one black juror (who voted for the defense), and the Sacramento trial, where large proportions of jurors of all racial backgrounds voted for the defense.

Male and female jurors also differed in their verdict preferences in the car accident cases. Specifically, 52.5% of women favored the plaintiff, compared to only 36.9% of men ($X^2<0.000$). A greater percentage of women voted for the plaintiff than did men in each of the individual mock trials. In only one of those trials (Marshall, TX) did the difference between the genders in verdict preferences fail to reach standard levels of statistical significance.

Jurors' verdicts in the prescription drug cases revealed a similar pattern of differentiation between jurors of different races and genders. In these cases, 64.4% of African-American jurors found for the plaintiff, compared to only 47.7% of white jurors ($X^2<0.000$). The only mock trial in which whites were more likely to find for the plaintiff was the Charleston, West Virginia case, but that was most likely due to the small number of African-American jurors (N=2) who participated in that mock trial. Men and women also differed in their verdicts of the prescription drug cases. Across all of the prescription drug mock trials, 52.2% of women favored the plaintiff, compared to 46.8% of men. While not a particularly large substantive difference, the difference is statistically significant ($X^2=0.006$). Moreover, in all but two of the nine mock trials, a greater percentage of women than men found for the plaintiff.

A first glance at the data from the accounting malpractice cases also show differences among jurors. Once again, African-American and white jurors saw the accounting malpractice cases differently, although the differences were not as striking as in the previous two cases. Overall, 48.2% of African-American jurors found for the plaintiff in trials against a major accounting firm, compared to only 35.7% of white jurors ($X^2<0.000$). In the seventeen mock trials that make up the data set, black jurors were more likely than whites to find for the plaintiff in all but three. However, in only three of these fourteen trials did the difference between black and white jurors reach the $X^2=0.05$ level of statistical significance. The lack of meaningful differences between jurors of different races in the accounting malpractice cases may be due in part to the relatively small numbers of African-American jurors in many of the mock trials. (For more information on the mock juries, see Appendix A.)

And while gender appeared to be an important factor in jurors' verdicts in the car accident and prescription drug cases, it seemed to matter much less in the accounting malpractice cases. Even across the entire sample of over 2,500 subjects, the differences between men and women remained small; 39.1% of women favored the corporate plaintiffs in their suits against a large accounting firm, compared to 35.7% of men (X^2=0.07). While women seemed to favor the plaintiff more than men in a handful of mock trials, in none of the seventeen trials did gender differences reach conventional levels of statistical significance.

While these results suggest that demographics may influence jurors' views of these cases, a simple cross-tabulation is not enough to support the conclusion that race or gender affect jurors' views of a case. Race is often correlated with other factors, including education and income. A juror's educational background or socio-economic status may affect her views of a case, and the apparent effects of race revealed through cross-tabulation may in fact be the result of differences in other, non-racial characteristics. To identify any effects of race on verdicts, one must control for the effects of these other variables. The next section presents a multivariate analysis of the effects of jurors' demographic and attitudinal variables on their verdicts.

Three Models of Juror Decision-Making

This section presents three multivariate models of juror decision-making. Each of the three models will be applied to the data from the three areas of civil litigation. In all of the models, the unit of analysis is the individual juror, and the dependent variable is the juror's verdict. The verdict variable has been coded as a 1 if the juror voted for the plaintiff, and a 0 if the juror voted for the defense. Because the dependent variable is dichotomous (that is, it takes one of only two possible values) logistic regression is used to estimate the effects of the independent variables on jurors' verdicts.

In Model 1, the independent variables include only jurors' gender and race. Gender is coded as a 1 for female jurors and a 0 for male jurors, while race has been split into dummy variables for African-American, Latino, Asian-American and white jurors. Note that the dummy variable for white jurors has to be omitted from the model to avoid over-specification. The regression coefficients for the race dummy variables can therefore be interpreted as the difference between the verdict preferences of white jurors and jurors from other racial backgrounds. Model 2 adds jurors' education, income and age to Model 1 (for more information on these demographic variables, see Appendix B). Finally, Model 3 adds three measures of jurors' attitudes to the demographic variables in Model 2. The first attitudinal variable measures jurors' political ideology, on a three-point liberal-conservative scale. Jurors who identified themselves as politically liberal are coded as a -1, jurors who claimed to be "middle of the road" are coded as a 0, and conservatives are coded as a 1. The other two attitudinal variable are indexes of jurors' attitudes toward business corporations and jurors' attitudes toward civil litigation. The business attitudes index is made up of five questions designed to measure the juror's views on corporations and government regulation of the economy. Each juror's index score is calculated by adding the juror's numerically-coded answers to the five questions that make up the index. The higher the juror's score, the more the juror believes in the need for government oversight of corporate activity. The litigation index is made up of jurors' responses to four questions about lawsuits and the state of the civil litigation system in America, and is also calculated for each juror by adding the juror's numerically-coded responses to the questionnaire items in the index. The higher the juror's score on the lawsuit index, the more the juror believes in litigation as a desirable and effective means of dispute resolution (for more information on the attitudinal variables, see Appendices A and B). To allow for comparison of the regression coefficients, all of the variables in each of the models have been re-scaled to range between zero and one.

All of the models also include dummy variables for each trial venue. These variables are intended to control for the slight variations in the evidence presented in each mock trial. There are also dummy variables in the models for whether the jurors lives in an urban, rural or suburban area. These variables are included as control variables and do not yield substantively interesting results, so the coefficients have not been reported here, but they are available from the author upon request.

RESULTS

The tables below include the results of the regression analysis. The entries are the "raw" logistic regression coefficients, and therefore have no immediate substantive interpretation. However, any positive coefficient indicates that as the value of that juror characteristic increases, the probability that the juror will find for the plaintiff also increases. A negative coefficient suggests that as the value of the characteristic increases, the probability of seeing a plaintiff verdict decreases. Note that re-scaling the variables to range between zero and one allows for a comparison of the coefficients and an approximation of the relative importance of each variable to the juror's verdict. Sample sizes and Negelkerke's R-squared statistics appear at the bottom of the table.

The Car Accident Cases

Table 2-1 shows the results of the three models of juror decision-making when applied to the car accident data. Model 1 shows that gender is a significant predictor of verdict, with women more likely than men to find for the plaintiff. Race is also important, but only to an extent. Latinos and Asians were statistically indistinguishable from whites. African-American jurors, on the other hand, were much more likely than jurors of other racial backgrounds to find for the plaintiff in these cases.

However, as previously mentioned, what may appear at first blush to be differences based on race can often be explained by differences in socio-economic factors, such as education or income. To test the hypothesis that the observed differences between jurors of different racial backgrounds are merely an artifact of differences in education or income, Model 2 includes those two variables, as well as age, as explanatory variables. The results of Model 2 reveal that, despite the inclusion of these additional factors, African-American and female jurors remain statistically different from other jurors. Although the size of the coefficients declined somewhat, race and gender remained significant predictors of verdict, and income proved to be a significant determinant of verdict as well, with wealthier jurors more likely than the poor to vote for the defendant.

Table 2-1: The Effect of Juror Factors on Verdicts in Car Accident Litigation

Juror Category	Model 1	Model 2	Model 3
Female	0.661*** (0.107)	0.647*** (0.109)	0.698*** (0.122)
African-American	1.409*** (0.289)	1.310*** (0.315)	0.931** (0.311)
Latino	0.162 (0.120)	0.179 (0.095)	-0.023 (0.072)
Asian-American	0.061 (0.346)	0.047 (0.333)	-0.108 (0.308)
Income	–	-0.858*** (0.239)	-0.692** (0.242)
Education	–	0.164 (0.252)	0.212 (0.213)
Age	–	0.271 (0.382)	0.348 (0.432)
Political Ideology	–	–	-0.528*** (0.064)
Business Attitudes	–	–	1.659*** (0.192)
Litigation Attitudes	–	–	1.006*** (0.130)
Constant	-1.053*** (0.261)	-0.925* (0.374)	-1.943*** (0.373)
Valid N Negelkerke R^2	1,423 0.208	1,362 0.223	1,320 0.267

* = Pr<0.05, ** = Pr<0.01, *** = Pr<0.001
Dependent variable is juror's verdict: 1=plaintiff, 0=defendant.
Cell entries are logistic regression coefficients. Robust standard errors are in parentheses.

Given that race and gender remain significantly related to verdicts despite the inclusion of education and income in the model, the remaining differences observed between African-Americans and other jurors, as well as those between men and women, may be a function of the different attitudes people from different backgrounds may have about the world. As discussed in Chapter 1, the "story model" of juror decision making suggests that the narratives jurors use to make sense of trial evidence are affected by their life experiences. Indeed, as shown in Table 2-2, the average scores on three measures of jurors' attitudes differ significantly between jurors of different races. These attitudinal differences may be driving the apparent differences between the races. For example, white jurors, on average, are more conservative, more pro-business and more pro-tort reform than other jurors. African-American jurors, on the other hand, tend to be the more liberal, more skeptical of big business and more accepting of litigation as a legitimate means of dispute resolution.

Model 3 therefore adds three attitudinal variables—jurors' political ideology, jurors' attitudes toward business and jurors' attitudes toward civil litigation—as explanatory variables in the model of juror decision-making. The results of Model 3 reveal that these attitudes all correlate significantly with verdict. The negative sign of the coefficient for political ideology suggests that more conservative jurors are more likely to find for the defense than liberal jurors. The positive sign of the coefficient for the business attitude index suggests that the more a juror distrusts big business, the more likely she is to find for the plaintiff. Similarly, the more a juror believes in civil lawsuits as an effective and positive means of dispute resolution, the more likely she is to find for the plaintiff.

Table 2-2: Attitude Differences between Jurors

Juror Race and Sample Size	Political Ideology	Business Attitudes	Litigation Attitudes
	The higher the score, the more conservative the juror. (Range = 0 to 1.)	The higher the score, the more the juror distrusts big business. (Range = 0 to 1.)	The higher the score, the more the juror supports litigation. (Range = 0 to 1.)
African Americans (N=1,483)	0.442	0.633	0.450
Whites (N=3,642)	0.552	0.559	0.260
Latinos (N=1,117)	0.495	0.589	0.339
Asian Americans (N=422)	0.461	0.596	0.317

Numbers are average attitude scores, by juror race.

However, including the attitudinal variables does not "explain away" all of the observed differences between men and women and between African-Americans and whites. While the size of the coefficient for African-American jurors declines once again from Model 2 to Model 3, African-Americans and females remain statistically distinguishable from other jurors, despite the inclusion of the socio-economic and attitudinal variables. In other words, if the only difference between men and women, and between black and white jurors, was in terms of education, income, political ideology or attitudes toward businesses and lawsuits, then we would expect the coefficients for race and gender in Model 3 to be zero.

Before discussing these finding further, let us first look at a different type of litigation to see if race and gender predict verdicts in only the car accident lawsuits, or if these juror factors remain significant predictors of verdict in other cases as well. The results from the prescription drug mock trials will show that the general findings about the importance of juror demographics and attitudes from the car accident data hold in a second type of civil litigation.

The Prescription Drug Cases

As before, the independent variables in Model 1 include only the juror's gender and race, and the results show that race is once again a significant predictor of verdict. However, as shown in Table 2-3, both Latino and African-American jurors have different verdict preferences from white jurors in the prescription drug data. Female jurors also appear to be more plaintiff-oriented than men, although the coefficient does not meet standard levels of statistical significance.

To test once again whether the observed effects of race are in reality a function of socio-economic differences, Model 2 adds the jurors' income, education and age to the determinants of their verdicts. As was the case in the car accident trials, while these variables reduce the size of the coefficients of the race variables, both Latino and African-American jurors appear to remain more "pro-plaintiff" than their white and Asian colleagues. Moreover, both education and income prove to be significant predictors of jurors' verdict preferences. In these prescription drug cases, as a juror's income and education increases, the probability that the juror will eventually vote for the defense also increases. The effect of education may be due to the nature of the evidence presented in this type of prescription drug litigation. Much of the defendant's case depends on sophisticated medical and epidemiological studies that challenge the plaintiffs' claims of a link between the medication and serious side effects. Jurors without a higher education may not value such evidence as much as more highly educated jurors.

Table 2-3: The Effect of Juror Factors on Verdicts in Prescription Drug Litigation

Juror Category	Model 1	Model 2	Model 3
Female	0.193	0.113	0.125
	(0.144)	(0.143)	(0.154)
African-American	0.838***	0.801***	0.484***
	(0.094)	(0.094)	(0.080)
Latino	0.310**	0.218*	0.058
	(0.114)	(0.105)	(0.095)
Asian-American	-0.027	-0.064	-0.193**
	(0.076)	(0.061)	(0.065)
Income	–	-0.624***	-0.440***
		(0.094)	(0.108)
Education	–	-0.514**	-0.382*
		(0.181)	(0.162)
Age	–	-0.081	0.191*
		(0.082)	(0.091)
Political Ideology	–	–	-0.420***
			(0.072)
Business Attitudes	–	–	1.854***
			(0.443)
Litigation Attitudes	–	–	1.085***
			(0.076)
Constant	-0.484***	0.150	-1.156***
	(0.079)	(0.137)	(0.304)
Valid N	2,589	2,478	2,450
Negelkerke R^2	0.077	0.095	0.159

* = Pr<0.05, ** = Pr<0.01, *** = Pr<0.001

Dependent variable is verdict: 1=liable, 0=not liable.

Cell entries are logistic regression coefficients. Robust standard errors are in parentheses.

Model 3 adds jurors' attitudes to the list of independent variables. And while the coefficient for Latino jurors drops to almost zero and loses its statistical significance with the inclusion of controls for jurors' attitudes, African-Americans remain distinguishable from other jurors. Moreover, Model 3 reveals that Asian-Americans are now significantly more likely than others to find for the defense, even when socio-economic and attitudinal factors are included in the model.[26] Income and education also remain significant, and all of the attitudinal variables show an effect similar to that observed in the car accident cases.

Although the particular demographic variables affecting verdict changed somewhat between the car accident and drug data sets, the effects of ideology and the attitude scales did not. All three of these variables are related to verdict in the prescription drug cases just as they were in the car accident cases, and the coefficients are of a similar magnitude. That is, more conservative jurors are more likely to vote for the defense, while jurors suspicious of big business and supportive of litigation are more likely to find for the plaintiff.

The car accident and prescription drug cases are similar in that they both involve an individual plaintiff suing a large corporate defendant. Both sets of lawsuit are also based on alleged defects in the company's product that led to serious personal injuries. The demographic and attitudinal findings discussed above may be particular to the nature of the legal conflict in these cases—that is, cases involving an individual seeking damages from a large business corporation to compensate them for an injury. Looking at juror decision-making in a third type of litigation—accounting malpractice—will provide a test of that hypothesis. Accounting malpractice involves a corporate plaintiff, as opposed to an individual plaintiff, suing another corporation, in this case, a large accounting firm, for alleged mistakes, oversights and other wrong-doing. The "injuries" claimed in the accounting cases are financial, as opposed to the physical injuries claimed by plaintiffs in the other two types of litigation. If jurors' characteristics correlate with their verdicts in accounting malpractice cases, we will have additional evidence that the non-findings in the literature on juror characteristics should be re-examined. If, on the other, hand, jurors' characteristics do not affect verdicts in the accounting cases, we will know that the general consensus in the literature may be correct, but that there may be an exception in some areas of civil litigation.

Accounting Malpractice Cases

The results in Table 2-4 bear many similarities to those from the previous two case types. Once again, Model 1 shows that female jurors favor the plaintiff somewhat more so than men, although the difference is small and not statistically-significant. Race, however, is once again an important determinant of jurors' verdicts. In these accounting cases, the verdict preferences of black and Latino jurors are statistically distinguishable from whites and from each other.

Model 2 adds education, income and age, and the results suggest that education has a substantively- and statistically-significant relationship with jurors' verdict decisions. Jurors with higher educational attainment and higher incomes are more likely to find for the defendant than are poorer or less educated jurors.

Table 2-4: The Effect of Juror Factors on Verdicts in Accounting Malpractice Litigation

Juror Category	Model 1	Model 2	Model 3
Female	0.115 (0.060)	0.100 (0.060)	0.103 (0.061)
African-American	0.453* (0.209)	0.410 (0.213)	0.364 (0.220)
Latino	0.313*** (0.089)	0.277** (0.105)	0.263* (0.105)
Asian-American	-0.406* (0.175)	-0.387* (0.181)	-0.391* (0.177)
Income	–	-0.049 (0.149)	0.044 (0.146)
Education	–	-0.221* (0.088)	-0.236** (0.088)
Age	–	-0.214 (0.198)	-0.104 (0.182)
Political Ideology	–	–	-0.111 (0.110)
Business Attitudes	–	–	0.515* (0.243)
Litigation Attitudes	–	–	0.173 (0.150)
Constant	-0.789*** (0.046)	-0.547*** (0.121)	-0.916*** (0.250)
Valid N	2,571	2,559	2,559
Negelkerke R^2	0.138	0.139	0.144

* = Pr<0.05, ** = Pr<0.01, *** = Pr<0.001
Dependent variable is verdict: 1=liable, 0=not liable.
Cell entries are logistic regression coefficients. Robust standard errors are in parentheses.

The addition of education and income also decreases the size of the coefficients for race, and diminishes the coefficient for black jurors to the point where black and white jurors are no longer distinguishable in terms of their verdict preferences. However, Latino jurors remain more plaintiff-oriented than whites, while Asian jurors appear to be more likely to find for the defense.

And as before, Model 3 adds jurors' political ideology, as well as their attitudes toward business and litigation, to the list of explanatory variables. As was the case in the previous two types of litigation, the addition of these variables fails to completely explain the observed differences in verdict preferences between jurors of different racial backgrounds. Of note in the accounting malpractice cases is the relatively small effect of these attitudes on jurors' verdicts. In the car accident and prescription drug cases, the attitudinal variables had by far the biggest effect on jurors' verdicts. In the accounting cases, only jurors' attitudes toward big business had a statistically significant relationship with their verdicts. While the sign of the coefficients for political ideology and litigation attitudes were positive just as they were in the previous cases, the coefficients were much smaller and did not reach standard levels of statistical significance.

INTERPRETING THE RESULTS

The results discussed above have relied on the "raw" logistic regression coefficients. Other than the sign of the coefficients and their relative sizes, these numbers have no substantive meaning. In order to understand the effects of these variables on jurors' verdicts, the coefficients must be transformed into verdict probabilities. This process is complicated somewhat by the fact that the effect of any one variable on verdict depends on the values of all of the other variables. In order to look at the effects of changes in one variable, the values of the other variables must be held constant, typically at their average values. The substantive effects of jurors' demographics and attitudes on their verdicts are presented below.

Car Accidents

Table 2-5 offers a substantive interpretation of the statistical findings presented in Table 2-1, above. Table 2-5 shows the changes in the probability of a juror finding for the plaintiff as the value of each explanatory variable changes, while holding all of the other variables constant at their means. For example, a female juror will find for the plaintiff approximately 49% of the time in these car accident cases, compared to an estimate of only 32% for men, when all of the other factors, such as education, income, age, attitudes, are set at their averages. Similarly, African-American jurors' likelihood of finding for the plaintiff is approximately 22 percentage points higher than for jurors of other racial groups. Wealthy individuals are more likely than poorer jurors to find for the defendant. Specifically, someone with a household income of less than $15,000 per year has an estimated probability of 47% of finding for the plaintiff, while someone with an income of over $75,000 per year has less than a 31% probability of finding for the plaintiff. These are large substantive differences, and directly challenge the findings in the literature that jurors' demographic characteristics have no effect on their verdicts in civil trials.

The power of the attitudinal variables to influence verdict is even more striking. On average, jurors who describe themselves as politically liberal are about 13 percentage points more likely than conservatives to find for the plaintiff in this type of car accident case, when all other variables are held constant at their means.

Table 2-5: Estimated Probability of a Plaintiff Verdict in Three Types of Civil Litigation

Juror Category	Case Type		
	Car Accident	Prescription Drugs	Accounting Malpractice
African American	54.6%	51.8%	–
Latino	–	–	37.4%
Asian American	–	37.5%	24.9%
White	32.2%	40.2%	32.1%
Female	49.1%	–	–
Male	32.4%	–	–
Income less than $15,000/year	47.0%	46.9%	–
Income more than $75,000/year	30.7%	36.2%	–
Less than high school education	–	46.3%	29.9%
Graduate degree	–	37.1%	25.2%
Politically Liberal	47.9%	47.3%	–
Politically Conservative	35.2%	37.1%	–
High Scorer (score=0.8) on the Business Regulation Index	47.3%	52.9%	34.9%
Low Scorer (score=0.2) on the Business Regulation Index	24.9%	27.0%	28.3%
Probability difference between scores of 0 and 1 on the Business Regulation Index	+36.3%	+41.6%	+11.1%
High Score (score=0.8) on the Litigation Attitudes Index	53.1%	55.4%	–
Low Score (score=0.2) on the Litigation Attitudes Index	38.2%	39.3%	–
Probability difference between scores of 0 and 1 on the Litigation Attitudes Index	+24.4%	+26.4%	

Entries are estimated probabilities of a plaintiff verdict with all other variables held constant at their means.
Cells with an "–" indicate that there were no statistically-significant results for that variable.

The substantive effects of the business attitude index are even larger: a person with a score of 0.2 on the business attitude index (that is, someone with a relatively low score on the 0 to 1 scale who is trusting of business and in favor of less government regulation of corporate activity) would find for the plaintiff only 24.9% of the time, while a person with a high score of 0.8 (that is, someone distrusting of businesses and in favor of greater government regulation of corporations) would find for the plaintiff an estimated 47.3% of the time. If one moves from the lowest score on the business attitudes index (zero) to the highest possible score (one), the probability of seeing a plaintiff verdict increases by over 36 percentage points.

One might expect that jurors' attitudes toward lawsuits would also have dramatic effects on their verdicts, and indeed this is the case. Someone with a negative view of lawsuits and who scores 0.2 on the lawsuit attitude index has an estimated probability of 38.2% of finding for the plaintiff. Contrast that with someone who scores 0.8 on the lawsuit attitude index, who would have an estimated probability of 53.1% of finding for the plaintiff. Moving between the two endpoints of the litigation index (from a score of 0 to a score of 1) results in a very large probability change of 24.4 percentage points.

One can also use the results from the logit regressions to calculate verdict probabilities for hypothetical jurors. For example, the most "plaintiff-oriented" person would be an African American woman who makes less than $15,000 per year, is politically liberal and has the highest possible scores on the business regulation and litigation indexes. Plugging these values into the model yields an estimated probability of 94% that such a person would find for the plaintiff if she served as a juror in a similar car accident trial. Contrast that hypothetical juror with a white male who makes over $75,000 per year, is politically conservative and has scores of zero on both the business regulation and lawsuit attitude indexes. The estimated probability that such a person would find for the plaintiff is approximately 3%. Of course, these are extreme examples; if such a person appeared for jury duty in a similar case, he or she would most likely be struck from the jury for cause. But, a more "average" person, say, a white female with the average income, education, ideology and attitude scores, would have an estimated 48% probability of finding for the plaintiff.

Prescription Drugs

Table 2-5 also shows the effects of juror characteristics on verdicts from the prescription drug cases. As was the case with the car accident data, African-American jurors are more likely to find for the plaintiff (51.8%) than are whites (40.2%) and Asian-Americans (37.5%) when all other variables are held constant at their means. People in the lowest income bracket are also more likely to find for the plaintiff (46.9%) than are the wealthiest jurors (36.2%). Education also affected verdicts in the prescription drug cases, as people without a high school diploma are more likely to find for the plaintiff (46.3%) than are people with graduate degrees (37.1%).

Political ideology and attitudes about businesses and litigation shaped jurors' verdicts in the prescription drug cases, just as they did in the car accident litigation. In fact, the substantive effects of those attitudes are even greater in the drug cases. For example, the size of the probability change associated with movement from one end of the business attitude index to the other is greater for the drug cases (41.6%) than for the car accident cases (36.3%). Similarly, the estimates of the total probability change as one moves from one end of the lawsuit scale to the other in the drug cases is 26.4%, compared to "only" 24.4% in the car accident cases. The differences between liberals and conservatives in terms of the probability of a plaintiff verdict were similar in both the car accident and prescription drug cases, with liberals approximately 12.7 percentage points more likely to find for the plaintiff in the car accident cases compared to a difference of 10.2 percentage points in the drug cases.

Accounting Malpractice

Table 2-5 also includes estimated probabilities of a juror finding for the plaintiff in the accounting malpractice cases. As in the other two areas of litigation, race matters. Asian-Americans seem to be the least likely to side with the plaintiff, with an estimated probability of only 24.9% of finding for the plaintiff when all other variables are held constant at their means. The estimated probability of a white juror finding for the plaintiff is 32.1% and Latinos 37.4%. Recall that in the final model of jurors' verdicts in the accounting malpractice cases, African-American and white jurors had the same verdict preferences.

Education was also an important factor in the accounting malpractice litigation. However, the substantive affects of education are relatively small, with the least educated jurors only 5 percentage points more likely than jurors with the highest education of finding for the plaintiff. The accounting cases differed from the other two types of litigation in that jurors' attitudes appeared to have relatively little impact on their verdict decisions. Only jurors' attitudes toward big business were statistically significant, and the substantive difference between jurors was not as large as the differences in the other two types of litigation. For example, moving between the two end points of the business attitude index in the accounting cases translated into a change in the probability of a plaintiff verdict of 11.8 percentage points. While not insignificant, this probability change is smaller than the estimates from the car accident and prescription drug data sets of 36.3 and 41.6 percentage points, respectively.

DISCUSSION

The empirical findings reported here suggest that juror factors—race in particular, but also gender, education and income—matter in these cases, as do jurors' attitudes toward issues relevant to the case. The effects are particularly strong in litigation involving an individual plaintiff. Why do jurors from different racial backgrounds react so differently to the same evidence? While the empirical results of this study may not suggest a clear answer to that question, they do help us eliminate some possibilities.

The models presented here control for many of the factors that often account for observed differences between different racial groups. What often appear to be differences between blacks and whites in a particular area of interest are often a function of differences in education, income, political orientation or some other factor. However, in this study, we can reject those factors as explanations for the observed differences in verdict preferences because the model includes and controls for those differences. Similarly, the model controls for any difference between jurors in terms of attitudes toward business corporations and the civil justice system. If the only differences between black and white jurors were their education, income, politics or attitudes, the inclusion of those variables should have "explained away" any variation between blacks and whites, and no significant relationship would have remained between jurors' race and their verdicts. Specifically, the coefficients for the race variables in the models should have dropped to zero. While the addition of education, income, politics and attitudes into the models did reduce the importance of race to below standard levels of statistical significance in some areas of litigation (Latinos in the prescription drug cases and blacks in the accounting malpractice cases) identifiable differences between racial groups remained in every model of juror decision-making.

The most likely explanation for the remaining difference between jurors of different races is that there are attitudes and beliefs not included in these models that affect verdicts. Some researchers have speculated that members of minority groups may be more likely than whites to side with the "underdog" or the "little guy" in civil lawsuits against big businesses, because of their personal experiences with racism and injustice at the hands of powerful groups and institutions. However, this hypothesis does not explain the effects of juror race on verdicts in the accounting malpractice cases. While black jurors' verdicts were not significantly different from those of whites in the final model of the accounting verdict decision, Latinos remained more likely to find for the plaintiff than others. In these cases, both parties are large, wealthy corporations, neither of which can be considered a "little guy" by nay stretch of the imagination. However, it is conceivable that some jurors may still associate with the plaintiff as a victim of injustice, even if the plaintiff is a large corporation.

Several other attitudes might also affect jurors' verdict decisions. Jurors' attitudes toward economic redistribution, social justice and punishment, among others, could conceivable color jurors' views of a civil lawsuit. Unfortunately the data available here do not include questions on these issues, so no empirical test of these hypotheses is possible. But now that a link between jurors' characteristics and their verdicts has been established, future research can attempt to identify the nature and scope of the attitudes that affect how jurors view civil lawsuits.

The results presented here also have obvious implications for jury selection at the beginning of civil trials. With enough information about the prospective jurors, attorneys in cases similar to these can use these models to calculate an estimated probability that a juror would find for the opposition. Knowing which jurors are statistically inclined to favor the opposition gives attorneys valuable information about how to use challenges for cause and peremptory strikes to remove the least sympathetic members of the jury. However, as the results above suggest, the least sympathetic jurors may also come disproportionately from one racial group. Concerned with time and juror privacy, judges often restrict the amount of information litigants can obtain through written or oral *voir dire* questions, so attorneys must often make jury selection decisions without knowing much about the attitudes and beliefs of the prospective jurors. Would striking jurors based on their race or gender—given that those easily observed traits may serve as rough proxies for attitudes—constitute unwanted and unfair discrimination, or an attorney simply trying to eliminate those jurors who are likely to be least sympathetic to her client's case? The following chapter will explore the issue of race and gender discrimination in jury selection and the Supreme Court's rulings on the legitimate use of the peremptory challenge.

CONCLUSION

This chapter challenges the consensus in the empirical literature on juror decision-making that jurors' characteristics have little or no effect on their verdicts in complex civil trials. Using large-sample data sets on decision-making by jurors in realistic mock trial settings, the results of this study present compelling evidence that jurors' demographics, including their race, gender, income and education, as well as their attitudes on case-relevant issues, can affect verdicts in three different types of civil litigation.

CHAPTER 3:

Discrimination, Conflicting Rights and the Peremptory Challenge: Understanding *Batson v. Kentucky*

With its 1986 decision in *Batson v. Kentucky*, the Supreme Court for the first time placed restrictions on the use of the peremptory challenge during jury selection. Prior to *Batson*, the peremptory challenge, or peremptory strike, allowed litigants to remove a certain number of prospective jurors from the panel without cause or even explanation. After *Batson* peremptory challenges based solely on the race of the prospective juror were no longer permitted. Following the initial *Batson* decision, the Court handed down a series of rulings concerning the peremptory challenge. However, these rulings have been inconsistent in terms of their effects on the peremptory; while some of the Court's decisions expanded *Batson's* reach, others seemed to loosen the previously established restrictions.

The *Batson* line of decisions also brought important changes to the Court's views of the jury. The first change was an abandonment of the Court's long-held belief that jurors' demographic characteristics could affect trial outcomes. The second was a shift in the Court's attention from protecting the rights of the accused to guaranteeing the rights of prospective jurors. The third change was a renewed concern with public confidence in the legitimacy of jury verdicts.

In practice, *Batson* has proven to be unwieldy, and according to its critics, largely ineffective in preventing race-based peremptory challenges. Previous commentary has recognized *Batson's* limitations and has also documented the changes in the Court's views of the jury within those cases. However, none of the research on the *Batson* line has put these elements together to understand fully the nature of the *Batson* line. What appear at first blush to be confusing and contradictory rulings on the peremptory challenge can instead be seen as an attempt by the Court to preserve the rights of both jurors and litigants. The effort to maintain both litigants' and jurors' rights is complicated by a conflict between them, as the rights of citizens not to be excluded from jury service because of their race or gender may come at the expense of litigants' rights to an impartial jury.

The first section of this chapter discusses the history of the Supreme Court's rulings on jury selection practices. Before the *Batson* decision, the Court's jurisprudence in this area, which spanned more than a century, revealed a concern for the rights of criminal defendants to the equal protection of the law and to a fair trial by an impartial jury. Within these cases, one can see the Court's belief that the composition of a jury can have a powerful effect on the outcome of a trial. The second section of the chapter discusses the *Batson* decision, its difficult implementation and its inconsistent progeny. The third section discusses the changes to the Court's views of the jury within the *Batson* line. Specifically, *Batson* brought a rejection of the Court's long-held belief that jury composition matters to jury verdicts, presented a new focus on the rights of citizens to serve as jurors, and showed the Court's heightened concern over public trust in the legitimacy of jury verdicts. The final section of the chapter attempts to bring these disparate elements of the *Batson* line together to argue that *Batson* is an attempt by the Court to guarantee the rights of jurors to be free from discriminatory jury selection practices, while also maintaining litigants' rights to a fair trial by an impartial jury.

SUPREME COURT RULINGS ON JURY SELECTION: 1879-1986

The Supreme Court's jurisprudence on questions of race and jury service dates back over a century. Over that period, the Court has consistently held that state actions that result in the systematic exclusion of racial and ethnic minorities from jury service violate a criminal defendant's equal protection rights under the Fourteenth Amendment.[27] This long line of cases began in 1879, when the Supreme Court in *Strauder v. West Virginia* struck down a state law allowing only white citizens to serve as jurors. The Court held that when blacks are systematically excluded from a jury, a black defendant no longer enjoys the equal protection of the law. In striking down the West Virginia statute, the *Strauder* Court recognized that criminal defendants have a strong interest in the racial composition of their juries, stating that:

> the statute of West Virginia, discriminating in the selection of jurors as it does, against Negroes because of their color, amounts to a denial of the equal protection of the laws to a colored man when he is put upon trial for an alleged offense against the State" (*Strauder v. West Virginia*, 1879, pg. 311).

The decision also recognized that the racial make-up of a jury could have a strong influence on its eventual verdict.

The *Strauder* Court took as a given that an all-white jury would view a case against a black defendant very differently than would a panel that included black citizens. The Court noted that:

> It is well known that prejudices often exist against particular classes in the community, which sway the judgment of jurors, and which, therefore, operate in some cases to deny to persons of those classes the full enjoyment of that protection which others enjoy" (*Strauder v. West Virginia*, 1879, pg. 310).

Although *Strauder* struck down state laws allowing only white citizens to serve on juries, southern states soon adopted other methods of blocking African Americans from jury service. One such method involved the use of different colored tickets to draw citizen's names for jury duty. The names of whites were written on white tickets, while the names of blacks were written on yellow tickets. After drawing the names, a court official gave the tickets to a clerk, who then "arranged" them into a final typed list of sixty names to be called as prospective jurors. Although many eligible black citizens lived in the areas in which this practice went on, none of them ever appeared on the jury list. The Court struck down the use of such colored tickets in *Avery v. Georgia* in 1953. A similar ploy relied on segregated tax returns to construct the lists from which citizens were called for jury duty. As was the case with the use of colored tickets, lists based on segregated tax returns were eventually challenged and ruled unconstitutional in *Whitus v. Georgia* (1967) and *Sims v. Georgia* (1967). When it became clear that the Supreme Court would not allow states to block black citizens from jury service, southern states grudgingly allowed the token inclusion of blacks on juries. Tokenism (defined as limiting African American representation on a jury to one person) was also challenged, and eventually abolished by the Court in the 1950 *Cassell v. Texas* decision. The Court even went so far as to overturn a conviction because of racial discrimination in the composition of the defendant's grand jury, even though the trial jury was properly selected (*Vasquez v. Hillery*, 1986).

Throughout all of these cases, as in *Strauder*, the Court maintained that it was the criminal defendant whose rights were violated by discriminatory jury selection procedures. In *Avery*, the case involving the colored tickets used to pick names for jury service, the Court ruled that if Jury Commissioners allowed the jury to be selected in a racially-discriminatory manner:

> th[e] conviction must be reversed—no matter how strong the evidence of petitioner's guilt. That is the law established by decisions of this Court spanning more than seventy years of interpretation of the meaning of "equal protection" (*Avery v. Georgia*, 1953, pg. 561).

And in *Cassell*, which struck down tokenism in jury selection, the Court wrote that, "Prohibiting racial disqualification of Negroes for jury service... has been consistently sustained and its violation held to deny a proper trial to a Negro accused" (*Cassell v. Texas*, 1950, pg. 288). Thus, well into the second half of the twentieth century, the Court continued to battle discrimination during jury selection, holding that such discrimination denied a black defendant the equal protection of the law.

Although the Court struck down state laws that prevented African Americans from appearing for jury duty, the Court refused to guarantee black representation on juries. Recognizing the difficulties of any attempt at racial proportional representation, the Court held that citizens enjoy no right to any particular jury composition. The

Court's rulings in effect stated that the composition of jury venires should be left to a random drawing of citizens' names, with every eligible person having the same probability of being chosen (*Cassell v. Texas*, 1950).

Also note-worthy in the jury discrimination decisions throughout this period is that the Court maintained its view that the racial composition of the jury was important to the outcome of the trial. As recently as the 1972 decision in *Peters v. Kiff*, in which the Court ruled that a defendant of any race may challenge a grand jury or jury venire from which blacks have been systematically excluded, the Court stated that:

> When any large and identifiable segment of the community is excluded from jury service, the effect is to remove from the jury room qualities of human nature and varieties of human experience, the range of which is unknown and perhaps unknowable. It is not necessary to assume that the excluded group will consistently vote as a class in order to conclude, as we do, that their exclusion deprives the jury of a perspective on human events that may have unsuspected importance in any case that may be presented (*Peters v. Kiff*, 1972, pg. 504).

Thus, a line of cases dating back to the *Strauder* decision in 1879 held that state practices that interfered with the race-neutral selection of names for jury service violated a defendant's right to the equal protection of the law under the Fourteenth Amendment. In these decisions the Court consistently opined that the racial composition of the jury mattered, as all-white juries were likely to see cases very differently than juries that represented all members of a community.

Gender and the "Fair Cross-Section" Cases

Another line of Supreme Court decisions has battled discrimination against women during jury selection. Instead of relying on the Equal Protection clause of the Fourteenth Amendment, these decisions are based on the Sixth Amendment right to a fair trial by an impartial jury. In *Taylor v. Louisiana*, the Court struck down laws limiting the participation of women on juries. The Court held that, "The requirement that a petit jury be selected from a representative cross section of the community, which is fundamental to the jury trial guaranteed by the Sixth Amendment, is violated by the systematic exclusion of women from jury panels" (*Taylor v. Louisiana*, 1975, pg. 522).

Just as the Court saw the importance of race in the *Strauder* line of cases, the "fair cross-section" cases reflected the Court's belief that the gender composition of a jury could also affect the outcome of a trial. For example, the case of *Ballard v. U.S.* involved the prosecution of a mother and son charged with mail fraud. Women had been excluded from the jury, and the defendants had appealed their conviction on the basis that they had been denied their right to trial by an impartial jury. In its decision, the Court suggested that men and women may see cases very differently, stating that:

> The truth is that the two sexes are not fungible; a community made up exclusively of one is different from a community composed of both; the subtle interplay of influence one on the other is among the imponderables" (*Ballard v. U.S.*, 1946, pg. 194).

In *Taylor*, the Court went so far as to suggest that the function of the jury as a guardian against government abuses may break down if certain groups are not allowed to participate, stating that the safeguard of the jury, "is not provided if the jury pool is made up of only special segments of the populace, or if large, distinctive groups are excluded from the pool" (*Taylor v. Louisiana*, 1975, pg. 531).

Swain v. Alabama and the Peremptory Challenge before 1986

Although the Court actively and consistently battled discrimination in the composition of grand juries and jury venires, it was unwilling until 1986 to limit the use of the peremptory challenge during jury selection. As a result, all-white (and all male) juries were the norm in many parts of the country, even though discrimination in the composition of jury lists was illegal. In other words, while black citizens could not be kept outside the courthouse doors, once inside, they were very often sent home through the attorneys' use of their peremptory challenges. In fact, jury selection manuals used by prosecutors often instructed them to strike blacks from criminal juries. These manuals were in use as late as the 1980s. The Dallas County District Attorney's Office published such guidelines, and their manuals have been used as evidence during the appeal of felony convictions (see, for example, *Miller-El v. Dretke*, 2005).

As late as 1965, the Warren Court ruled in *Swain v. Alabama* that peremptory strikes used to remove all of the black veniremen from a jury were not impermissible under the Constitution. The case involved jurors assembled to hear the case against a black man accused of rape. The all-white Alabama jury convicted the defendant and sentenced him to death. Writing for the Court, Justice White explained that the unrestricted use of peremptory challenges was needed to achieve an impartial jury:

> Alabama contends that its system of peremptory strikes—challenges without cause, without explanation and without judicial scrutiny—affords a suitable and necessary method of securing juries which in fact and in the opinion of the parties are fair and impartial. This system, it is said, in and of itself, provides justification for striking any group of otherwise qualified jurors in any given case, whether they be Negroes, Catholics, accountants or those with blue eyes. Based on the history of this system and its actual use and operation in this country, we think there is merit in this position (*Swain v. Alabama*, 1965, pp. 211-12).

While it may surprise some to see the Court best known for its ruling in *Brown v. Board of Education* unwilling to end the often-discriminatory use of peremptory challenges, the *Swain* Court ruled that peremptory challenges were needed to guarantee litigants' right to an impartial panel under the Sixth and Seventh Amendments. According to the *Swain* Court, if that meant striking all of the black citizens from a jury, so be it.

In upholding the constitutionality of race-based peremptories in *Swain*, the Court maintained its view that group membership brought with it certain perspectives, and that peremptory strikes based on those assumptions were permissible because they resulted in impartial juries. The Court stated that:

> For the question a prosecutor or defense counsel must decide is not whether a juror of a particular race or nationality is in fact partial, but whether one from a different group is less likely to be. It is well known that these factors are widely explored during the voir dire, by both prosecutor and accused. This Court has held that the fairness of trial by jury

> requires no less (*Swain v. Alabama*, 1965, pp. 220-21).[28]

Thus, an examination of the Supreme Court's century-long effort to end racial (and later, gender) discrimination in jury selection reveals three consistent ideas about the jury within the Court's decisions. The first is that the racial and gender composition of a jury may affect its eventual verdict. The second is that jury discrimination cases are questions of litigants' rights (in most cases, those of criminal defendants) and that litigants enjoy neither the equal protection of the law nor the right to a fair and impartial jury when citizens are systematically excluded from jury service solely because of their race or gender. The third is that the litigants' belief in the impartiality of the jury is vital to the acceptance and legitimacy of the verdict. Twenty years after *Swain*, the Court would re-examine the use of the peremptory challenge, and in so doing, turn these three ideas upside-down.

The Supreme Court and the Peremptory Challenge under *Batson*

Twenty years after *Swain*, the Court revisited the question of race-based peremptory challenges. In 1986, the Court in *Batson v. Kentucky*[29] effectively reversed the *Swain* precedent and ruled that a prosecutor's use of peremptory challenges to remove black veniremen from a jury violated the Equal Protection rights of not only the defendant but also the stricken jurors.[30] Additional restrictions on the use of the peremptory challenge followed.

In 1991, the Court handed down *Edmonson v. Leesville Concrete Company*, which expanded *Batson's* ban on race-based peremptories in criminal trials to the parties involved in civil litigation. *Edmonson* involved a black construction worker who sued his employer for negligence after sustaining a workplace injury. During jury selection, the defendant company used two of its three peremptory challenges to remove black jurors from the panel. The plaintiff objected, citing *Batson.* The court overruled the objection, pointing out that *Batson* applied only to state prosecutors in criminal trials. On appeal, the Supreme Court reversed the decision of the lower court, and thereby included civil trials within the jury selection rules established under *Batson.*

The following year, the Court outlawed race-based peremptories made by criminal defendants in *Georgia v. McCollum.* That case involved the trial of three white defendants charged with assaulting a black couple. The defense attorney admitted that he planned to strike all of the black jurors from the panel and the prosecution objected. The trial court upheld the strikes, as did the Georgia Supreme Court, but upon review, the U. S. Supreme Court reversed.

The Court has expanded the list of prohibited peremptories to include other groups. *J.E.B. v. Alabama* banned strikes based on gender. In *J.E.B.*, prosecutors struck all of the male jurors in a paternity and child-support case against a male defendant. The all-female jury found that the defendant was the father and therefore owed child support to the mother. On appeal, the Court ruled that peremptory strikes made solely on the basis of gender, like those based solely on race, violated the Equal Protection Clause of the Fourteenth Amendment. The Court's 1991 ruling in *Hernandez v. New York* extended *Batson* protections to Latinos. And in *Powers v. Ohio*, the Court decided that any litigant, regardless of race, may make a *Batson* claim. *Powers* involved a white defendant who objected to the State's peremptory strikes against black jurors. Lower courts have expanded *Batson* protections to Jews, Italians, whites and Native Americans. Table 3-1 lists the *Batson* line of cases.

Table 3-1: The Expansion of *Batson*

J.E.B. v. Alabama ex rel. T.B. 511 U.S. 127 (1994) Extended *Batson* restrictions to strikes based on gender.
Georgia v. McCollum 505 U.S. 42 (1992) Extended *Batson* rules to strikes made by criminal defendants.
Edmonson v. Leesville Concrete Company 500 U.S. 614 (1991) Extended *Batson* rules to parties in civil lawsuits.
Hernandez v. New York 500 U.S. 352 (1991) Extended *Batson* restrictions to strikes based on ethnicity.
Powers v. Ohio 499 U.S. 400 (1991) Any defendant, regardless of race, may make a *Batson* objection.
Allen v. Hardy 478 U.S. 255 (1986) The *Batson* ruling is not retroactive.
Batson v. Kentucky 476 U.S. 79 (1986) Outlawed peremptory challenges based solely on a juror's race.

Batson in Practice

After the Court announced the *Batson* decision, some commentators predicted a quick end to the peremptory challenge (see, for example, Bray, 1992; Cressler, 1992 and Leach, 1994-1995). Since then, most observers have argued that peremptory challenges—even those based on race and gender—live on due to the weak and inconsistent enforcement of the *Batson* rules (see, for example, Cavise, 1999; Diamond, Ellis and Schmidt, 1997-1998; Mililli,

1996; Charlow, 1997-1998; Swift, 1992-1993 and Pizzi, 1987).

A *Batson* challenge to a peremptory strike involves a three-step process. A litigant wishing to challenge one or more of the opposition's strikes must first demonstrate a prima facie case of discrimination in the use of those peremptories.[31] If a prima facie case is established, the attorney who made the challenged strike must offer a race-neutral (or gender-neutral, as the case may be) explanation for the peremptory. Finally, in step three, the judge must decide whether the challenged peremptory was the result of purposeful race or gender discrimination.

Although the Court outlined the three steps of a *Batson* challenge, the ruling left the standards to be used during each of the three steps only vaguely defined. The Court seemed unwilling to specify a particular process for a *Batson* challenge, writing, "We decline… to formulate particular procedures to be followed upon a defendant's timely objection to a prosecutor's challenge" (*Batson v. Kentucky*, 1986, pg. 99). The Court also failed to prescribe a remedy for a *Batson* violation. The *Batson* decision mentions two possible remedies, but endorses neither of them (*Batson v. Kentucky*, 1986, pp. 99-100). One possible remedy is to replace the entire venire and repeat the jury selection process. However, replacing the entire venire might give attorneys a perverse incentive to make discriminatory peremptory strikes, in the hopes that the second group of prospective jurors might be more sympathetic to their case than the first. The other option is to reinstate the illegally-stricken juror. However, this option raises questions about the impartiality of that juror, as the reinstated juror will probably have witnessed her dismissal, and perhaps hold a grudge against the litigant who struck her (Cavise, 1999, pg. 543-4 and Brown, 1998-1999).

Because of the lack of clear direction concerning the enforcement of the *Batson* decision, lower courts have had to establish their own *Batson* procedures. This has led to procedural inconsistencies between courts (Marder, 2006, pp. 1707-8). In his research on lower courts' implementation of the *Batson* rules from 1986 to 1993, Mililli identified at least eight different standards in use by lower courts for establishing a prima facie case of discrimination during the first stage of a *Batson* hearing. The eight different methods range from a judge simply ensuring that a "sufficient number" of minorities sit on a jury, to more sophisticated analyses that compare the percentage of peremptory challenges used against minority citizens with the percentage of minorities in the jury venire (Mililli, 1996, pp. 471-2). Melilli found that in most *Batson* hearings, the court accepted both the prima facie case of discrimination and the neutral explanations given for the strikes. While a prima facie case of discrimination was successfully established in 62% of *Batson* hearings, a successful neutral explanation was then offered in 78% of those cases. As a result, while most litigants who raised a *Batson* objection were able to show prima facie discrimination, the court eventually sustained the objection only 17% of the time. Ironically, Mililli found that *Batson* challenges were most likely to be successful when the objection was raised against the elimination of white jurors from the panel. In those cases, the *Batson* objection was sustained 53% of the time (Mililli, 1996, pp. 460-4).

Raphael and Ungvarsky also looked at the neutral explanations given for peremptory strikes in the second step of a *Batson* hearing. Looking at over 2,000 *Batson* hearings conducted between 1986 and 1992, Raphael and

Ungvarsky found that only a very small percentage of neutral explanations were rejected by judges. In fact, the only "explanations" that were rejected were most often no explanation at all or the attorney actually admitting that the strike was based on the juror's race. Raphael and Ungvarsky found twelve common categories of race-neutral explanations—including the juror's prior experience with the criminal justice system, age, occupation, marital status, demeanor, education, socio-economic status and religion, among others—that judges almost always accepted as explanations for what had appeared to be race-based peremptory challenges. The ease of overcoming *Batson's* "neutral explanation" stage is exemplified by the fact that, "there are a number of cases in which courts accepted as a neutral explanation the prosecutor's statement that she struck a juror because, among other reasons, the juror was black" (Raphael and Ungvarsky, 1994, pg. 236).

Almost ten years went by after the original *Batson* decision before the Supreme Court gave some guidance on the implementation of *Batson*. The Court's short *per curiam* opinion in *Purkett v. Elem* weighed in on the nature of an acceptable "race neutral" explanation during the second step of a *Batson* hearing, and the Court's ruling came as something of a shock. *Purkett* involved peremptory strikes used by the State to remove two black jurors from a Missouri robbery trial. When the defense objected to the strikes, citing *Batson*, the prosecutor offered the following, now-infamous, "race neutral" explanation:

> I struck [juror] number twenty-two because of his long hair. He had long curly hair. He had the longest hair of anybody on the panel by far. He appeared to be not a good juror for that fact, the fact that he had long hair hanging down shoulder-length, curly, unkempt hair. Also he had a moustache and

> goatee type beard. And juror number twenty-four also has a moustache and goatee type beard. Those are the only two people on the jury... with facial hair... And I didn't like the way they looked, with the way the hair is cut, both of them. And the moustaches and the beards look suspicious to me (*Purkett v. Elem*, 1995, pg. 765).

When Purkett's appeal reached the High Court, the prosecutor's strikes were upheld. The Court stated that race-neutral explanations need be only that—race-neutral—and that the explanation need not be "persuasive or even plausible" (*Purkett v. Elem*, 1995, pg. 768). The Court stated that:

> The prosecutor's proffered explanation in this case—that he struck juror number 22 because he had long, unkempt hair, a moustache, and a beard—is race-neutral and satisfies the prosecution's step 2 burden of articulating a nondiscriminatory reason for the strike" (*Purkett v. Elem*, 1995, pg. 769).

Even before *Purkett*, a common criticism of *Batson was* that it did not go far enough to eliminate the discriminatory use of the peremptory challenge. Attorneys wishing to use their peremptory challenges as they saw fit could concoct almost any explanation for their race- and gender-based strikes (see Marder, 2006 and Page, 2005). The *Purkett* decision seemed to sanction and even encourage such behavior, and, according to critics, effectively pulled any teeth *Batson* had left. Cavise noted that, following *Purkett*, "Only the most overtly discriminatory or impolitic lawyer will be caught in *Batson*'s toothless bite and, even then, the wound will be only superficial" (Cavise, 1999, pg. 501). Even some members of the Court recognized the apparent message of *Purkett*. In their *Purkett* dissent, Justices Stevens and Breyer wrote:

> Today, without argument, the Court replaces the *Batson* standard with the surprising announcement that any neutral explanation, no matter how 'implausible or fantastic,' even if it is 'silly or superstitious,' is sufficient to rebut a prima facie case of discrimination (*Purkett v. Elem*, 1995, pg. 775).

The dissent quoted the Missouri Supreme Court ruling on another *Batson* case, in which that court had refused to allow implausible race-neutral explanations for challenged peremptories (*Missouri v. Antwine*, 1987).[32] The Missouri high court wrote:

> We do not believe, however, that *Batson* is satisfied by 'neutral explanations' which are no more than facially legitimate, reasonably specific and clear. Were facially neutral explanations sufficient without more, *Batson* would be meaningless. It would take little effort for prosecutors who are of such a mind to adopt rote 'neutral explanations' which bear facial legitimacy but conceal a discriminatory motive. We do not believe the Supreme Court intended a charade when it announced *Batson*" (Quoted in *Purkett v. Elem*, 1995, pg. 774, Justices Stevens and Breyer, dissenting).

In reducing *Batson* to a "charade," the *Purkett* decision seemed to mark the end of the Court's experiment in limiting litigants' use of the peremptory challenge. The ten-year expansion of the *Batson* line to cover civil litigants, criminal defendants and prosecutors, as well as strikes based on gender and ethnicity, was reduced in *Purkett* to nothing more than a mild procedural hassle for attorneys wishing to use their peremptory challenges as they saw fit. Cavise argued that *Purkett*, "marked the definitive retrieval of the peremptory challenge from the endangered species list and, with no more than a whimper, it marked the final demise of the *Batson* doctrine into the role of useless symbolism" (Cavise, 1999, pg. 528). Justice Breyer also commented on the anemic state of *Batson* after *Purkett*:

> At *Batson's* first step, litigants remain free to misuse peremptory challenges as long as the strikes fall *below* the prima facie threshold level. At *Batson*'s second step, prosecutors need only tender a neutral reason, not a "persuasive, or even plausible" one. And most importantly, at step three, *Batson* asks judges to engage in the awkward, sometime hopeless, task of second-guessing a prosecutor's instinctive judgment—the underlying basis for which may be invisible even to the prosecutor exercising the challenge (*Miller-El v. Dretke*, 2005, Justice Breyer, concurring).

Following *Purkett*, the Court did not hear another case concerning the use of the peremptory challenge for ten years. One might have viewed this long period of inattention as a signal that the Court was willing to let the weakened *Batson* precedent wither and die. However, the Court once again reversed course, and in 2005 began to hand down rulings apparently intended to give *Batson* new life.

That year, the Supreme Court handed down two decisions affecting *Batson* hearings. In the first, *Johnson v. California*, the Court held that California's standard for evaluating a prima facie case of discrimination in the first step of a *Batson* hearing was too restrictive. California had required attorneys raising a *Batson* objection to show a "strong likelihood" of discrimination in the use of the strikes. Under *Johnson,* the Court ruled that an "inference" or even "suspicion" of discrimination was enough to establish a prima facie case of discrimination. The Court therefore struck down California's more demanding requirement. Marder saw *Johnson* as an "effort to maintain *Batson's* integrity" and as a "successful defense of *Batson* from one of the more onerous burdens imposed upon objectors to the exercise of a peremptory challenge" (Marder, 2006, pp. 1699-1700). In the second 2005 case, *Miller-El v. Dretke,* the Court overturned a murder conviction older than *Batson* itself. The Court rejected a "neutral" explanation given by the prosecutor for a peremptory strike used against a black juror because the explanation given also applied to white jurors who were not stricken. The decisions in *Johnson* and *Miller-El* made a prima facie case of discriminatory peremptories easier to establish, and, more importantly, may encourage lower courts to give greater scrutiny to the explanations offered for challenged strikes.

The most recent Supreme Court ruling in the *Batson* line also speaks to the evaluation of the "neutral explanations" given for suspect peremptory challenges. In March of 2008, the Court decided *Snyder v. Louisiana,* holding that the judge in Snyder's first-degree murder trial erred when he allowed the prosecutor's peremptory challenge of a black juror. The justices' vote was 7 to 2 and Justice Alito delivered the opinion of the Court. Justices Thomas and Scalia dissented.

The juror at the heart of the *Snyder* case, Mr. Jeffrey Brooks, was a student teacher at the time of jury selection and initially explained to the court that jury duty would be a hardship for him because it would interfere with his teaching requirements. However, the court contacted the dean at Mr. Brook's school and received permission for him to make up any missed work. Nonetheless, the following day, the prosecutor struck Mr. Brooks. When defense counsel objected, the prosecutor explained the reason for his strike:

> Number 1, the main reason is that he looked very nervous to me throughout the questioning. Number 2, he's one of the fellows that came up at the beginning [of *voir dire*] and said he was going to miss class. He's a student teacher. My main concern is for that reason, that being that he might, to go home quickly, come back with guilty of a lesser verdict so there wouldn't be a penalty phase. Those are my two reasons. (*Snyder v. Louisiana*, 2008, pg. 5-6).

The Supreme Court reviewed both of these explanations and concluded that they were unpersuasive.

The first explanation, that Mr. Brooks seemed nervous, was rejected by the Court because it was unclear from the trial transcripts whether or not the judge relied on that explanation when ruling on the *Batson* objection. The judge made no comment on the reasons for allowing the strike after the prosecutor offered his explanations, stating only, "All right. I'm going to allow the challenge. I'm going to allow the challenge" (*Snyder v. Louisiana*, 2008, pg. 5). The Court argued that:

> the trial judge may not have recalled Mr. Brooks' demeanor. Or the trial judge may have found it unnecessary to consider Mr. Brooks' demeanor, instead basing his ruling completely on the second proffered justification for the strike. For these reasons, we cannot presume that the trial judge

credited the prosecutor's assertion that Mr. Brooks was nervous (*Snyder v. Louisiana*, 2008, pg. 6).

The Court then considered the second reason offered by the prosecutor for the strike, that Mr. Brooks' desire to get back to work would prevent him from considering a verdict that would require an additional penalty phase of the trial. The Court pointed out that Mr. Brooks seemed satisfied when informed that the dean would "work with him" to make up any missed student teaching. The Court also pointed out that other jurors had more pressing work and family conflicts that would certainly make them eager to avoid a lengthy trial, yet these jurors were not stricken by the prosecutor. Having rejected both of the prosecutor's justifications, the Supreme Court held that, "the explanation given for the strike of Mr. Brooks is by itself unconvincing and suffices for the determination that there was *Batson* error" (*Snyder v. Louisiana*, 2008, pg. 5). Table 3-2 lists these recent rulings clarifying the three stages of a *Batson* hearing.

Table 3-2: Clarifying *Batson*?

Snyder v. Louisiana 552 U.S. ___ No. 06-10119 (2008) Speculative juror hardships are "unconvincing" reasons for a challenged peremptory.
Miller-El v. Dretke 545 U.S. 231 (2005) Race neutral explanations for a challenged peremptory are not permissible if they also apply to jurors who were not struck.
Johnson v. California 545 U.S. 162 (2005) California's standard for establishing a prima facie case of a discriminatory peremptory is struck down as too restrictive.
Purkett v. Elem 514 U.S. 765 (1995) "Long hair" and "goatee beards" are acceptable race-neutral explanations for a challenged peremptory.

How the decision in *Snyder* will affect jury selection remains to be seen. One could argue that the Court's criticism of the prosecutor's "unconvincing" explanations means that attorneys must now present explanations of their challenged strikes that are not only race-neutral, but also "convincing." The Court's heavy reliance on the trial transcripts in its opinion may also encourage trial judges to make very clear the reasons for their *Batson* rulings. On the other hand, *Snyder* may simply re-affirm *Miller-El*, in which the Court held that an explanation for a challenged strike will fail if the explanation also applies to a juror who was not stricken.

But clearly the history of the *Batson* line of cases follows an unusual, see-saw progression. Between 1986 and 1994, the Court first established and then broadened restrictions on the use of the peremptory challenge. In 1995, however, *Purkett v. Elem* seemed to alter the Court's direction, effectively de-clawing the *Batson* decision by allowing almost any race-neutral explanation for a challenged peremptory strike. *Purkett* might have meant the end of *Batson*, but for the most recent rulings, including *Miller-El* and *Snyder*, which are apparently intended to give *Batson* new life.

One might wonder if changes to the membership of the Court could explain these shifts in the *Batson* line. While the replacement of old members with new ones of different political or ideological stripes can lead to changes in doctrine and precedent, the changes in the Court's membership between 1986 and 2008 do not account for the inconsistency in the *Batson* line of cases. While the membership of the Court changed dramatically in that twenty-two year period (only Justice Stevens heard all of the cases from *Batson* through *Snyder*), the votes on cases concerning peremptory challenges did not. In none of the cases was the decision closer than 6 to 3. Because the votes on the *Batson* line did not change significantly with changes to the composition of the Court, we can reject the hypothesis that the see-saw progress of the *Batson* line is the result of any ideological changes in the justices sitting on the High Court.

THE COURT'S CHANGING VIEWS OF THE JURY UNDER *BATSON*

As discussed above, the Supreme Court's rulings on discriminatory jury selection practices prior to *Batson* revealed a Court concerned primarily with the rights of criminal defendants to the equal protection of the law. These rights were violated by discriminatory jury selection practices, because the racial and gender composition of a jury could have an important impact on the outcome of a trial. With its rulings in the *Batson* line of cases, however, the Court reversed many of its long held beliefs about the jury. The Court also shifted its attention toward protecting the rights of prospective jurors.

Juror Factors and Verdicts Under *Batson*

The *Batson* line marked a shift away from the Court's long-held belief that the demographic composition of a jury could affect the outcome of a trial. Throughout the *Batson* line of cases, the Court has consistently rejected the idea that the racial, ethnic or gender composition of a jury could have any effect on its verdict. In *Batson*, the Court dismissed as an "assumption" any link between jurors' race and their verdicts:

> Although a prosecutor ordinarily is entitled to exercise peremptory challenges for any reason, as long as that reason is related to his view concerning

> the outcome of the case to be tried, the Equal Protection Clause forbids the prosecutor to challenge potential jurors solely on account of their race or on the assumption that black jurors as a group will be unable impartially to consider the State's case against a black defendant (*Batson v. Kentucky*, 1986, pp. 79-80).

In *Allen v. Hardy*, in which the Court stated that the *Batson* rules on the use of peremptory strikes were not retroactive, the Court implied that the race of the members of the jury had no impact on their verdict. *Batson* would not be retroactive because eliminating race-based peremptories, "does not have such a fundamental impact on the integrity of fact-finding as to compel retroactive application" (*Allen v. Hardy*, 1986, pg. 256).

The Court's new view on the lack of any relationship between jurors' demographics and their verdicts continued throughout the *Batson* line. In *Edmonson*, which brought civil litigants under the *Batson* rules, the Court again rejected any relationship between race and verdict, and argued that only two explanations exist for a race-based peremptory challenge:

> Whether the race generality employed by litigants to challenge a potential juror derives from open hostility or from some hidden and unarticulated fear, neither motive entitles the litigant to cause injury to the excused juror (*Edmonson v. Leesville Concrete Company*, 1991, pg. 631).

And in *J.E.B*, the Court outlawed peremptory challenges based on gender, and again rejected any possible link between jurors' gender and their verdicts:

> Respondent's rationale—that its decision to strike virtually all males in this case may reasonably have

> been based on the perception, supported by history, that men otherwise totally qualified to serve as jurors might be more sympathetic and receptive to the arguments of a man charged in a paternity action, while women equally qualified might be more sympathetic and receptive to the arguments of the child's mother—is virtually unsupported and is based on the very stereotypes the law condemns (*J.E.B. v. Alabama ex rel. T.B.*, 1994, pg. 127).

In summarizing the rationale for its decision in *J.E.B.* the Court concluded that:

> the Equal Protection Clause prohibits discrimination in jury selection on the basis of gender, or on the assumption that an individual will be biased in a particular case for no reason other than the fact that the person happens to be a woman or happens to be a man (*J.E.B. v. Alabama ex rel. T.B.*, 1994, pg. 148).

The Court's rejection in the *Batson* line of any role for juror characteristics in verdict outcomes is not unanimously supported among the justices. The dissenters in the *Batson* line of cases have continued the Court's long-held position that jurors' characteristics may influence trial outcomes. In his *Batson* dissent, Justice Rehnquist wrote:

> Common human experience, common sense, psychological studies and public opinion polls tell us that it is likely that certain classes of people statistically have predispositions that would make them inappropriate jurors for particular kinds of cases" (*Batson v. Kentucky*, 1986, pg. 122, Justice Rehnquist, dissenting).

And in her concurring opinion to *J.E.B.*, Justice O'Conner concedes that gender may indeed affect verdicts in some cases:

> In extending *Batson* to gender, we have added an additional burden to the state and federal trial process, taken a step closer to eliminating the peremptory challenge, and diminished the ability of litigants to act on sometimes accurate gender-based assumptions about juror attitudes (*J.E.B. v. Alabama*, 1994, pg. 152, Justice O'Conner, concurring).

Several observers have commented on the shift in the Court's views within the *Batson* line on the relationship between jurors' demographics and their verdicts. Muller argues that, "By the time the Court decided *J.E.B. v. Alabama ex rel. T.B*, it was not merely announcing that race and gender do not rationally predict juror perspective, but preaching that view with a vengeance" (Muller, 1997, pg. 102). King also noticed a shift, pointing out that:

> the Court's views on the empirical question [of how jurors' demographics affect their verdicts] are hopelessly inconsistent. … For many decades, the Court has assumed that jury discrimination affects jury decisions, but in some of its most recent opinions it has abandoned this position (King, 1993, pg. 64).

She continues, "The Supreme Court seems unable to decide whether jury discrimination affects jury decisions" (King, 1993, pg. 67).

Dismissing any role for race and gender in juror's verdict preferences under *Batson* also presents the Court with a paradox. Muller points out that if race does not affect verdicts, then removing blacks from the panel should not affect the outcome of a trial. Because the outcome of the trial is not affected, a *Batson* violation should not require any legal remedy. Muller also notes that the justices who dissented in *Batson* were also those who continued the Court's recognition that jurors' characteristics might affect their verdict decisions. Muller concludes that, "This then is the full paradox of *Batson*: the Justices who *would* find harm in a *Batson* violation *cannot*; the Justices who *can* find harm in a *Batson* violation *will not*" (Muller, 1997, pg. 96).

Why then did the Court find it necessary to completely alter its opinion on the importance of juror traits in *Batson*? Despite his detailed analysis of the *Batson* line, Muller has no answer and states only that, "It has never been entirely clear why *Batson's* proponents have clung so tenaciously to the view that race and gender are not just illegal but irrational proxies for viewpoint" (Muller, 1997, pg. 131). As will be argued below, such a "color blind" position is critical to an understanding of the Court's intentions under *Batson*.

The New Focus on Jurors' Rights under *Batson*

The *Batson* Court's altered views on the effect of jurors' demographics on their verdicts was not the only major change in its jury selection jurisprudence. The *Batson* line also saw a shift in the Court's attention away from the rights of criminal defendants and toward those of prospective jurors (see, for example, Stoltz, 2006 and Underwood, 1992). As discussed above, jury selection cases prior to *Batson* emphasized the importance of securing a defendant's rights to the equal protection of the law and a fair trial by an impartial jury. The *Batson* line, in contrast, increasingly focused on the rights of citizens not to be excluded from jury service because of their race or gender. While the Court recognized as long ago as *Strauder* that criminal defendants were not the only parties with interests in non-discriminatory jury selection, and that prospective jurors also had a stake in the fair selection of juries, the focus of the Court prior to *Batson* remained squarely on the rights of criminal defendants to the equal protection of the law.

Each of the cases in the *Batson* line illustrates the Court's new focus on the rights of citizens not to be unfairly excluded from jury service. The *Batson* opinion stated, "By denying a person participation in jury service [through the use of a peremptory challenge] on account of his race, the State…unconstitutionally discriminates against the excluded juror" (*Batson v. Kentucky*, 1986, pg. 80). In *Powers v. Ohio*, the Court's decision begins with a discussion of the violation of jurors' rights that occurs when prosecutors make race-based peremptory challenges:

> the State's discriminatory use of peremptories harms the excluded jurors by depriving them of a significant opportunity to participate in civil life (*Powers v. Ohio*, 1991, pg. 400).

Edmonson contains similar language: "Race-based exclusion of potential jurors in a civil case violates the excluded persons' equal protection rights" (*Edmonson v. Leesville Concrete Company*, 1991, pg. 614). And in *Georgia v. McCollum*, the Court explained that:

> whether it is the State or the defense who invokes them, discriminatory challenges harm the individual juror by subjecting him to open and public racial discrimination (*Georgia v. McCollum*, 1992, pg. 42).

Barbara Underwood argues that the Court's new focus in the *Batson* line on the rights of excluded jurors is the proper one, as jurors are the primary victims of the discriminatory use of peremptory challenges. She writes:

> In 1986, *Batson v. Kentucky* foreshadowed the Court's renewed interest in the rights of the excluded jurors, mentioning them as part of the description of the manifold evils of jury discrimination. Finally, in the 1991 cases of *Powers* and *Edmonson*, the Court gave the excluded jurors the place they deserve at the foundation of jury discrimination law (Underwood, 1992, pg. 744-5).

She contends that the attention previously paid by the Court in its jury discrimination decisions to the rights of criminal defendants was somewhat misguided, as that rights claim depended on the idea that race could affect a jury's verdict. She argues that:

> the defendant's stake in race-neutral jury selection is highly speculative, because the ban on jury discrimination may or may not affect the racial composition of the jury, and the racial composition of the jury may or may not affect the verdict (Underwood, 1992, pg. 745).

Other commentators have criticized the Court's focus on the rights of jurors. Stoltz argues that litigants' rights should be valued more highly than jurors':

> After all, the defendant is without question the focal point of any criminal prosecution. He will be subject to highly concrete and personal harm if the jury finds him guilty, so it does not seem logical to subordinate his rights to those of prospective jurors, whose potential harm is much less imminent and perhaps somewhat nebulous (Stoltz, 2006, pg. 1045).

While one can argue whose rights—jurors or litigants'—are more important, the argument is intimately related to perceptions of the jury and how best to maintain public confidence in the jury and the justice system as a whole.

The Court's Concern with Jury Legitimacy

A third major change discernable in the *Batson* line is the Court's concern with maintaining public confidence in the jury system. As discussed above, jury discrimination cases prior to *Batson* focused on the rights and perceptions of litigants, whose belief in the fairness of jury verdicts was undermined by racial discrimination during jury selection. While the legitimacy of jury verdicts was certainly a concern of the Court prior to *Batson*, it is only in the recent line of cases on the peremptory challenge that the Court has openly and explicitly expressed a desire to bolster public confidence in the jury system. According to the *Batson* line, only by eliminating the discriminatory use of the peremptory challenge can the public's belief in the legitimacy of jury verdicts be maintained. For example, in the original *Batson* decision, the Court wrote:

> The harm from discriminatory jury selection extends beyond that inflicted on the defendant and the excluded juror to touch the entire community. Selection procedures that purposefully exclude black persons from juries undermine public confidence in the fairness of our system of justice (*Batson v. Kentucky*, 1986, pg. 88).

In *Edmonson*, the majority opinion held that, "racial discrimination in jury selection casts doubt on the integrity of the judicial process" (*Edmonson v. Leesville Concrete Company*, 1991, pg. 615). The *Edmonson* Court even argued that, "Racial bias mars the integrity of the judicial system, and prevents the idea of democratic government from becoming a reality" (*Edmonson v. Leesville Concrete Company*, 1991, pg. 628). In *J.E.B.*, the Court also pointed out the damage that discriminatory jury selection procedures could cause to public confidence in the justice system:

> The community is harmed by the State's participation in the perpetuation of invidious group stereotypes and the inevitable loss of confidence in our judicial system that state-sanctioned discrimination in the courtroom engenders (*J.E.B. v. Alabama*, 1994, pg. 141).

And in *Georgia v. McCollum*, the Court wrote that, "discriminatory challenges…harm the community by undermining public confidence in this country's system of justice" (*Georgia v. McCollum*, 1992, pg. 42).

The Court's emphasis on the public's views of the jury system in *Batson* further distanced the Court from its pre-*Batson* focus on the interests and rights of litigants. Whereas the Court had previously concentrated on guaranteeing the equal protection and fair trial rights of litigants in its pre-*Batson* jurisprudence, the *Batson* Court's attention to public perceptions of the jury system marked a sharp change of course.

UNDERSTANDING *BATSON V. KENTUCKY*

The peremptory challenge presented the *Batson* Court with a dilemma. On the one hand, over a century of legal opinion had been dedicated to ending racial and gender discrimination during jury selection, and the unrestricted use of the peremptory challenge made race and gender discrimination possible, and even common. On the other hand, the peremptory challenge, according to the precedent set in *Swain*, was an invaluable tool for seating impartial juries. A clash of rights claims seemed inevitable. On the one side were minority citizens with the right to be free from state-sanctioned racial discrimination, which remained possible as long as litigants wielded the peremptory challenge. On the other side were parties to criminal trials and civil lawsuits, with the right to a fair trial by an impartial jury, which, according to *Swain*, could only be achieved if the litigants were allowed the unfettered use of their peremptory challenges.

In the *Batson* line, the Court has attempted to walk a tight rope between these two positions. The Court's decisions attempt to preserve both the rights of citizens to be free from discrimination and the rights of litigants to an impartial jury. To do this, the Court needed to 1) reject any role for juror demographics in verdicts, 2) change its previous focus from the rights of litigants to those of citizens and the public at large, and 3) temper the *Batson* line in such a way that the protection of the rights of jurors never severely infringed on the rights of litigants, and vice versa.

In order to accomplish this difficult balancing act, the Court had not only to reverse *Swain*, but also to alter several of its previous statements about the workings of the jury. As discussed above, the first of these new assertions was that juror demographics have nothing to do with trial outcomes. This effectively eliminated litigants' argument that an impartial jury required the use of race- and gender-based peremptory challenges. If race and gender do not affect verdicts, then litigants are not harmed by any Court-imposed limitations on their race- and gender-based peremptory challenges. Litigants maintain their right to an impartial jury, because race, gender and ethnicity, according to the Court, do not affect jurors' views of a case. The Court even attempted to head off claims of a conflict of rights with powerful rhetoric appealing to a color-blind ideal:

> A prohibition against the discriminatory exercise of peremptory challenges does not violate a [litigant's] constitutional rights. It is an affront to justice to argue that the right to a fair trial includes the right to discriminate against a group of citizens based on their race (*Georgia v. McCollum*, 1992, pg. 43).

Dismissing any role for race or gender in jurors' verdicts allowed the Court to appear to end race- and gender-based discrimination in the use of peremptory strikes at no cost to the rights or interests of litigants.

However, the Court's claims about a lack of any relationship between the composition of a jury and its verdict ring hollow. The link between jurors' demographic characteristics and their verdicts is not a matter of constitutional or legal interpretation, but is instead an empirical question. Simply stating that race and gender do not matter to verdicts does not necessarily make it so, even if you are a Supreme Court justice. Intuition suggests that the race and gender of the members of a jury may make a great deal of difference to the outcome of certain types of trials, and the findings of Chapter 2 lend empirical support to that intuition. Also, if the discriminatory use of peremptory challenges is really an "affront to justice" why not eliminate the peremptory entirely?[33]

Because the Court may sense the weakness of its claims about the irrelevance of juror demographics to verdicts, simply denying such a link is not enough to achieve the Court's goal of maintaining the rights of both jurors and litigants. Another step that allows the Court to avoid sacrificing litigants' rights when limiting the use of the peremptory challenge is to shift its focus to the rights of citizens to serve on juries. Had the Court in the *Batson* line maintained its long history of focusing on the rights of litigants, one would naturally ask why the litigants should not be allowed to have some control over the composition of their juries, when the Court had for so long held that jury composition is critical to a fair trial by an impartial jury. So the Court consciously turned the focus of the *Batson* line toward the protection of citizens' rights to be free from racial and gender discrimination during jury selection. The Court's renewed concern over threats to public confidence in the legitimacy of jury verdicts found throughout the *Batson* line also speak to this shift away from the rights of litigants.

But the *Batson* line stopped well short of guaranteeing a citizen the right to serve, or of abolishing the peremptory challenge entirely. To ensure that litigants' rights to an impartial jury were also protected, the Court made *Batson* inherently difficult to enforce. The Court only recently began to outline standards for the three steps of a *Batson* hearing. Lower courts have been forced to establish their own methods of adjudicating *Batson* disputes. Yet this confusion serves a purpose, because *Batson's* procedural ambiguity allows the Court to have its cake and eat it, too. The spirit and rhetoric of the century-long line of anti-discrimination cases remain in *Batson*, as do the appearance of Court-mandated procedures designed to prevent discrimination. Yet the decision does not go so far as to severely limit the day-to-day use of the peremptory challenge.

Even the progress of the *Batson* line reflects the Court's desire to acknowledge anti-discrimination goals without placing excessive limitations on the peremptory challenge. The history of the *Batson* line shows that the Court quickly expanded *Batson* to include strikes made by civil litigants and criminal defendants, and also prohibited strikes based on gender and ethnicity. But the Court then hollowed out these already-thin decisions with its ruling in *Purkett v. Elem*. Recently, however, perhaps sensing that it had gone too far in weakening *Batson*, the Court reinstated some procedural hurdles to race- and gender-based peremptories with its decisions in *Johnson*, *Miller-El* and *Snyder*. The Court has attempted a delicate balance with a line of decisions that, at least in spirit, furthers its long anti-discrimination legacy, but in reality maintains litigants' power to exercise control over the composition of their juries. *Batson* attempts to recognize both citizens' legitimate claims to equal participation in the administration of justice, regardless of race or gender, as well as litigants' rights to an impartial jury.

CONCLUSION

The twenty-year history of *Batson v. Kentucky* reveals a pattern of expansion and contraction of restrictions on the use of peremptory challenges during jury selection. After placing the first limits on the use of the peremptory in *Batson*, the Court expanded the scope of prohibited challenges and applied them to civil as well as criminal litigants. However, the Court then chose to severely limit any power *Batson* had in its 1995 *Purkett* decision, allowing almost any "race-neutral" explanation for a peremptory challenge. Why would the Court expand *Batson* and then dramatically limit its enforcement? And if the Court wanted to let *Batson* protections fade, why reinvigorate *Batson* as it did with its rulings in *Johnson*, *Miller-El* and *Snyder*?

The *Batson* line also brought dramatic changes in the way the Court views the jury. The Court rejected its long-held belief that the demographic composition of a jury might affect its verdict, and also abandoned its focus on the rights of litigants to the equal protection of the law and an impartial jury. Instead, the *Batson* Court concentrated on the rights of citizens not to be excluded from jury service because of their race and gender, and repeatedly expressed concern with maintaining public confidence in the legitimacy of jury verdicts. Why did the Court find it necessary to make these radical changes under *Batson*?

The answers to these questions lie in the realization that there is a trade-off in limiting the use of the peremptory challenge. The see-saw history of the *Batson* line and the Court's altered views on the jury within those decisions are best understood as an attempt by the Court to moderate *Batson's* effects. The unwieldy *Batson* decision and its inconsistent progeny allow the Court to continue the spirit and rhetoric of the century-long battle against discriminatory jury selection practices, but without sacrificing the peremptory challenge as a method of empanelling what litigants consider to be impartial juries.

CHAPTER 4:

What's Going on in There? Jury Deliberations and Trial Outcomes

The analysis in Chapter 2 showed that jurors' characteristics and attitudes can have a significant impact on their verdict decisions. However, a jury verdict is not an individual decision, but rather a product of a jury's group deliberations. Jurors must discuss the case with each other and try to reach a verdict. The extent to which the process of deliberation affects the outcome of jury trials is of considerable interest to observers of the jury system. The secretive nature of jury deliberations also contributes to a natural curiosity about what goes on behind the closed doors of the deliberation room.

This chapter will look at the nature and effects of jury deliberations. The first section of the chapter will offer a brief look at the literature on the function of jury deliberations and the effects of deliberations on jury verdicts. The next section will offer a glimpse inside the deliberation room. Data drawn from post-trial interviews with the members of eleven civil juries will offer a better understanding of how deliberations are conducted and what effects deliberations have on the outcome of a trial. Analysis of this data will show that several factors, including the size of the competing juror factions, the first-ballot vote during deliberations, and even the demographics of the members of the jury, may affect jury decision-making. A statistical analysis of the data also supports a common argument in the literature that deliberations may exert a "leniency bias" on jury verdicts.

WHY DELIBERATE?

Why require juries to deliberate? Why not simply poll the members of the jury or take a secret ballot vote after the litigants have presented their closing arguments? The literature on jury deliberations suggests that the process of discussing and debating the issues of a trial has beneficial effects on juror decision-making. Specifically, deliberations correct individual jurors' factual errors about the case and forge a shared consensus on the proper outcome of the trial.

During jury deliberations, individual jurors present their arguments for their preferred verdicts. However, individual jurors may incorrectly recall the information presented during the trial, or may have misunderstood the significance of a particular piece of evidence. Research has shown that one of the biggest advantages of the deliberation process is that deliberations help to eliminate jurors' factual errors. Hastie, Penrod and Pennington found that individual jurors, when tested, were able to accurately answer about 60% of the questions posed to them about the case evidence they had heard. When jurors came together as a group, however, "jury memory averages over 90 percent correct for evidentiary material and over 80 percent correct for information from the judge's instructions" (Hastie, Penrod and Pennington, 1983, pg. 81).

Ellsworth reported similar results after she found that jurors who took part in deliberations scored higher on a test of factual knowledge about a case than did jurors who did not deliberate. She found that on a multiple-choice test of factual issues:

> jurors performed quite well, answering correctly an average of 8.8 out of fourteen questions (there were four response alternatives, so 3.5 correct answers would be expected by chance). Jurors also performed better than those subjects who did not deliberate (Ellsworth, 1989, pg. 218).

Deliberations reduced errors because jurors with a mistaken understanding of the evidence were challenged and then corrected by their fellow jurors. Ellsworth reported that:

> Questions regarding the distance and angle of vision of the various witnesses were generally resolved correctly, and errors of fact generally were corrected. None of the jurors maintained an erroneous perception of an important case fact after the hour of deliberation (Ellsworth, 1989, pg. 217).

Deliberations also forge jurors' individual beliefs about the case into a group consensus. Deliberations expose jurors to different perspectives on the case and jurors share their stories about what they believe took place. In her study on the effects of jury deliberations, Ellsworth found that the consensus that emerged was not simply an average of the individual jurors' diverse perspectives. Instead, extreme views or "implausible scenarios are generally weeded out" during deliberations (Ellsworth, 1989, pg. 223). As a result, jurors gain an understanding of the case that is, "more complete and more accurate than any of the separate versions that contributed to it, or indeed than their average" (Ellsworth, 1989, pg. 206). More than simply correcting factual errors, the process of deliberations transforms the jury into a decision-making body greater than the sum of its parts. Jonakait concurs with this view on the benefits of jury deliberations. He writes that a deliberating jury, "has the potential to transcend the intellectual and experiential limitations of each of its members" (Jonakait, 2003, pg. 47).

Jury Deliberations and Verdicts

While deliberations may serve to correct factual errors and forge a consensus, it is not clear from the literature that jury deliberations have much of an impact on the outcome of the trial. Several researchers have concluded that verdicts are very often the product of a powerful "majority effect," in which the majority opinion among the individual jurors after closing arguments determines the jury's eventual verdict. For example, in their study of jury behavior, Kalven and Zeisel reported that in approximately 90% of jury trials, the results of the "first ballot" vote taken by the jury—that is, the majority position at the beginning of deliberations—predicted the jury's eventual verdict (Kalven and Zeisel, 1966).[34] In another study of jurors in felony criminal trials, Sandys and Dillehay found that juries with a first-ballot majority in favor of a guilty verdict eventually found the defendant guilty in 151 of 160 trials, or 94% of the time. Similarly, of 49 trials in which the first-ballot majority favored acquittal, the jury acquitted the defendant 37 times, or 76% of the time (Sandys and Dillehay, 1995).

Juries deliberating on civil trials appear to follow a similar pattern. Schkade, Sunstein and Kahneman compared jurors' pre-deliberation punitive awards with the eventual awards of six-person mock juries told to find a unanimously-acceptable punitive damages award (Schkade, Sunstein and Kahneman, 2002). Schkade *et al.* found that if a majority of the individual jurors awarded no punitive damages before deliberations, the jury as a whole eventually awarded punitive damages only 4% of the time. And if a majority of jurors wanted to award some level of punitive damages before deliberations, the jury as a whole agreed to award punitive damages 98% of the time.

These studies of both criminal and civil juries suggest that "come from behind" wins, or a single juror swaying the rest of the jury with impassioned arguments, may make for great drama, but happen very rarely in the real world. Jurors in the minority typically change their minds, acquiesce to the majority position, or are simply out-voted if the verdict does not require a unanimous decision.[35] Kalvan and Zeisel draw an analogy to illustrate the relative unimportance of deliberations:

> The deliberation process might well be likened to what the developer does for an exposed film: it brings out the picture, but the outcome is predetermined (Kalven and Zeisel, 1966, pg. 498).

Not only is the first ballot vote often predictive of the eventual verdict, but the size of the majority is also important. Hastie, Penrod and Pennington found that as the size of the majority faction increased, the probability that jurors in the minority would change their votes also increased (Hastie, Penrod and Pennington, 1983). Jurors in large majorities were also extremely unlikely to change their votes. Jurors in a faction of ten or more switched sides less than 5% of the time. Kerr and MacCoun found a similar pattern in their mock jury experiments, reporting that no juror changed sides when belonging to a faction of ten or more jurors (Kerr and MacCoun, 1985, pg. 355. See also Tindale, *et al.*, 1990).

Hastie *et al.* also identified an influence of the decision rule on the probability of a juror changing sides. The more restrictive the decision rule, that is, the larger the majority needed to reach a verdict, the more likely jurors in the minority were to eventually switch sides. In trials requiring a unanimous verdict, a single hold-out juror eventually came over to the majority position over 75% of the time. If only super-majorities of ten or eight jurors were required, the probability of a single hold-out juror changing sides dropped significantly, to 59% and 38%, respectively (Hastie, Penrod and Pennington, 1983, pg. 106). The reason for these differences is clear: jurors whose votes are needed to avoid a hung jury face considerable social pressure to come over to the majority position, whereas jurors whose votes are not needed can stick to their position without interfering with the jury's ability to render a verdict.

While the "majority effect" has been well documented in the jury decision-making literature, deliberations are not simply the aggregation of jurors' pre-deliberation verdict preferences. In fact, there is evidence to suggest that jury deliberation (and other forms of group decision-making) can lead to collective decisions quite different from a simple aggregation of the individual group members' pre-deliberation preferences. Research on group behavior has revealed "group polarization" and "choice shift" effects during collective decision-making. Group polarization refers to differences between individuals' preferences before and after the discussion, while choice shift refers to the difference between the group's eventual decision and the average of the individual preferences at the beginning of discussions (see Zuber, Crott and Werner, 1992 and Isenberg, 1986).

When applied to jury decision-making, choice shifts and polarization effects can result in a "leniency bias" in criminal verdicts. The leniency bias refers to a well-documented advantage enjoyed by the defense during deliberations in criminal trials. For example, MacCoun and Kerr found that juries that were evenly split between conviction and acquittal at the beginning of their deliberations acquitted the defendant significantly more than

50% of the time (MacCoun and Kerr, 1988). Specifically, they reviewed thirteen studies of jury decision-making and found that among juries that began deliberations evenly split and that were able to reach a verdict (that is, the jury did not hang) the jury acquitted the defendant approximately 80% of the time. In other words, these studies showed that "acquittal was about four times as likely as conviction for initially split juries that reach a verdict" (MacCoun and Kerr, 1988, pg. 23).

MacCoun and Kerr conducted another study in which they found that among 22 twelve-person mock juries that were evenly split 6-6 at the beginning of deliberations, only one jury eventually voted to convict the defendant. Of the other juries, nine voted to acquit and 13 "hung" because they could not reach a verdict in the time allotted for deliberations. A similar pattern emerged among evenly split six-person juries. Of the 28 six-person juries in the study, only three eventually voted to convict, while thirteen voted to acquit and twelve hung (Kerr and MacCoun, 1985, pg. 355). MacCoun and Kerr have also looked at the voting behavior of juries with 2/3 majorities at the beginning of deliberations. Of those juries with a 2/3 majority favoring conviction at the beginning of deliberations, the jury eventually handed down a guilty verdict at a proportional rate of 67%. However, in those juries with a 2/3 majority in favor of acquittal, the defendant was eventually found not guilty 94% of the time (MacCoun and Kerr, 1988, pg. 23). Davis et al. (1988) report finding a similar leniency bias.

MacCoun and Kerr attribute the leniency bias to the high burden of proof required in criminal trials. The researchers hypothesized that the need for proof "beyond a reasonable doubt" gave jurors favoring acquittal a rhetorical tool they could use during deliberations for raising doubts in the minds of pro-conviction jurors. The leniency bias may also be a function of social and legal norms that prefer acquitting the guilty to convicting the innocent.

If the burden of proof accounts for the leniency bias in criminal trials, one would expect to see a greatly reduced leniency bias, if any at all, in civil trials, where the plaintiff must prove her case only by a "preponderance of the evidence." However, in their studies of mock civil juries deliberating on punitive damages awards, Schkade, Sunstein and Kahneman also reported choice shifts. These shifts were much larger than would be expected if the only factor driving the phenomenon was the burden of proof. The authors showed fifteen different trials to a sample of mock jurors. After hearing about the cases, jurors were asked how much they believed the defendant deserved to be punished in each case on a scale from 0 to 8. Jurors were also asked how much they would award in punitive damages in each case.

Having made their individual determinations, jurors were then assigned to juries and were instructed to deliberate to a unanimous verdict. At the end of the deliberations, the jury as a whole was asked to once again determine how much the defendant deserved to be punished and how much the jury would award in punitive damages. The researchers found that the effect of deliberations depended on whether or not individual jurors judged the defendant to be deserving of high punishment or low punishment. In cases with average pre-deliberation punishment ratings of 5 or higher (on a scale from 0 to 8), the jury's collective punishment rating after deliberations tended to be higher than the mean of the individual jurors' pre-deliberation ratings. For cases with average punishment ratings of 4 or lower, the jury's punishment rating tended to be lower than the average of the individual jurors' punishment ratings. Schkade *et al.* described these results as, "systematic *choice shifts*, in which deliberation generally increases differences among cases, by making severe verdicts more severe and lenient verdicts more lenient, relative to the pre-deliberation judgments of jurors" (Schkade, Sunstein and Kahneman, 2002, pg. 51). Schkade *et al.* attribute these choice shifts during deliberations to rhetorical and social advantages enjoyed by those advocating a majority position. They argue that informational and normative processes push groups toward a more extreme version of the majority preference:

> When a group is inclined in a certain direction, most of the publicly expressed arguments will be made in the same direction, thus heightening people's sense that the original tendency makes sense. Social influences matter, too. People do not want to be seen as mildly disapproving of conduct that most people find abhorrent, or of being severely disapproving of conduct that most people do not greatly mind (Schkade, Sunstein and Kahneman, 2002, pg. 58).

In other words, those individuals arguing for a popular position are likely to have a good deal of support for movement toward their preferred outcome, in terms of both arguments made and social pressures within the group.[36]

Another possible factor influencing jurors' views during deliberations is the jurors' personal characteristics. Hastie, Penrod and Pennington asked mock jurors to evaluate their fellow jurors' persuasiveness during deliberations on a scale from 0 to 5, and found that several individual characteristics, including education, income, social status and occupational status, correlated with a juror's perceived persuasiveness (Hastie, Penrod and Pennington, 1983). A juror's persuasiveness was also highly correlated with the amount a juror spoke during deliberations, as well as the number of arguments made and the pieces of evidence cited by the juror (Hastie, Penrod and Pennington, 1983). Another study found that jurors with high prestige occupations, such as professionals, seemed to have a greater influence during deliberations than jurors with lower-status occupations (Strodtbeck and Mann, 1956).

Sommers found evidence that the racial make-up of the jury can also affect the deliberation process (Sommers, 2006). He found that racially diverse juries exchanged a wider range of information during their deliberations than all-white juries. In fact, Sommers found that the effects of diversity were most pronounced on white jurors. White jurors who deliberated with black jurors cited more case facts, were more accurate in their recall of the case, and were more open to discussions of the effects of race on criminal defendants than were the members of all-white juries. In fact, just the prospect of deliberating with a heterogeneous group seemed to affect white jurors' judgments, as white jurors in diverse groups were more lenient toward black defendants in their pre-deliberation verdicts than were white jurors who knew they would be part of an all-white deliberation panel. Sommers attributes these effects to an increased salience of racial issues for white jurors confronted with diverse groups. The heightened salience of race activated white jurors' desire to avoid any appearance of racial prejudice, and this desire compelled white jurors to entertain a broader spectrum of issues than they would have in an all-white environment.

THE DATA

To test the findings in the literature about the effects of deliberations on jury verdicts, data were collected from actual jury deliberations of eleven civil trials conducted between 2000 and 2005. While each trial is unique, these eleven trials shared many similarities. All of the trials involved lawsuits brought by an individual plaintiff against a major auto-maker. The lawsuits were based on allegations of defects in the design of the vehicles that led to severe accidents and injuries. In its defense, the auto makers claimed that the vehicles were safely designed and contained no defects and that driver error caused the accident and resulting injuries. Ten of the eleven trials involved claims stemming from high-speed rollover accidents, and the eleventh trial involved a fire that erupted in a vehicle after a high-speed rear-end collision.

Soon after each trial, the jurors were contacted by telephone and asked to answer a few questions about their experiences on the jury. Of the 130 jurors involved in the eleven trials, interviews were conducted with 87 jurors. The other 43 jurors could not be interviewed for a variety of reasons. Some were contacted but refused to participate in an interview. However, most of the jurors who were not interviewed could not be reached, either because no correct telephone number could be found for them or because the juror was away from home during the period the interviews were conducted. During each interview, the juror was asked questions on a variety of topics, including the juror's individual verdict decision and the main reasons for that decision. Jurors were also asked about the deliberation process. Specifically, jurors were asked about any jurors who changed their votes during deliberations and the reasons the jurors gave for those changes. Each interview lasted between twenty minutes and two hours. Additional information about the juries' deliberations, such as the gender and racial composition of the jury, the length of the jury's deliberations, and the jury's eventual verdict, were provided by the trial attorneys. Table 4-1 summarizes the data on the interviews.

These data have several advantages over data drawn from mock jury deliberations. The jurors in these eleven trials had to render a real verdict in a real case, as opposed to acting as if they were real jurors in a mock trial simulation. While mock jurors typically take their decisions very seriously,[37] there is no substitute for the real thing, particularly when studying jury deliberations. Researchers must often place limitations on mock jury deliberations, particularly in terms of time. For example, Schkade *et al.* limited their jury deliberations to 30 minutes (Schkade, Sunstein and Kahneman, 2002). Because Kerr and MacCoun studied juries' reactions to nine different cases, they were forced to limit their juries' deliberations on each case to only 10 minutes (Kerr and MacCoun, 1985). Allowing unrestricted time for mock juror deliberations is rare (see, for example, Kaplan and Miller, 1987). Of course, a real jury faces no time limit for its deliberations. Indeed, some of the juries in this sample deliberated for a week before reaching their verdicts.

Table 4-1: Summary of Data from Post-Trial Juror Interviews

Trial Location	Jury Size	Juror Interviews	Female Jurors	Non-White Jurors	First Vote (Plaintiff: Defense)	Jurors Changing Sides During Deliberations	Final Verdict (Plaintiff: Defense)	Hours of Deliberations
San Antonio, TX	12	10	8	4	6:6	4	2:10	20
Cleveland County, OK	12	8	7	1	0:12	0	0:12	9
Anaheim, CA	12	7	9	2	5:7	2	3:9	56
San Bernardino, CA	12	9	4	6	1:11	2	3:9	56
Oklahoma City, OK	12	11	7	2	3:9	0	3:9	2.5
Denver, CO	10	7	5	0	2:8	2	0:10	16
Houston, TX	12	8	8	1	1:11	0	1:11	2.5
St. Clair County, IL	12	7	6	3	3:9	3	0:12	2
San Joaquin, CA	12	9	10	4	2:10	2	0:12	3
Santa Barbara, CA	12	5	6	1	6:6	4	2:10	7
Alameda, CA	12	6	6	3	8:4	1	9:3	32
TOTALS	**130**	**87**	**76**	**27**		**20**		

It should be noted that few if any social science data sets are perfect, and these data are no exception. These data suffer from several problems. The sample size is rather modest (N=130), although not atypical for studies that rely on data drawn from post-trial juror interviews (for more on the problems associated with data from post-trial juror interviews, see the discussion on the relative merits of different data sources in Chapter 1). While 87 jurors were interviewed, information on the remaining 43 is taken from the recollections of the other jurors who were interviewed. This information comes second-hand, but was substantiated in every case by several jurors, who all had similar recollections about which jurors favored each side, and which jurors, if any, changed their minds during deliberations. While getting information second hand is certainly not ideal, the information collected on the jurors who were not interviewed is not difficult for other jurors to recall and substantiate. Jurors easily remember which jurors supported each side, as jurors spend hours if not days discussing the case with each other and often take several votes a day to see if anyone has changed his or her position. In all of these trials, votes were taken by a show of hands, so all of the jurors knew how the vote stood at various points during the deliberations and which jurors favored each side. A juror changing sides during deliberation is also a very important development for the jury and is therefore easy for jurors to recall.

However, in order to identify any differences between those jurors who were interviewed and those who were not, a statistical comparison of the two groups of jurors was conducted. Table 4-2 shows the results of this comparison. The proportions of female and non-white jurors were similar in both the interviewed and non-interviewed groups. In fact, the group of interviewed jurors had slightly higher proportions of women and minorities. The only significant difference between the two groups was in the jurors' first ballot vote. The interviewed jurors were less likely to start deliberations as plaintiff jurors (only 22% were plaintiff jurors at the beginning of their deliberation) while the non-interviewed group had a higher proportion (44%) of plaintiff jurors (p=0.03).

Table 4-2: Comparison of Interviewed and Non-Interviewed Jurors

	Non-Interviewed Jurors (N=43)	Interviewed Jurors (N=87)
Jury Foreman	0.05	0.10
Female Juror	0.51	0.62
Non-White Juror	0.19	0.22
Juror's First-Ballot Vote was for Plaintiff*	0.44	0.22
Juror changed sides during Deliberations	0.19	0.14

* = Difference in means is statistically significant (p=0.03).
Cell entries are means.

However, as mentioned above, jurors' recollections of which jurors favored each side are typically very accurate, and are substantiated by several jurors in each case, so there is little chance that jurors' first-ballot votes may be incorrectly categorized. The trials in this data set deal exclusively with litigation against auto-manufacturers. The data are therefore by no means a random sample of all civil trials. However, the types of trials studied here raise issues similar to most product liability claims and are therefore not unusual or idiosyncratic.

Another concern with the data set is its lack of information on several factors that may affect a juror's decision to change her vote during deliberations. For example, there is no way to know or to quantify how committed the jurors were to their positions at the beginning of deliberations. Some jurors may have been less certain about their verdict than others, and jurors' relative uncertainty could contribute to their decision to change sides during deliberations. Because of these limitations in the data, any findings from their analysis should be taken as a quick and preliminary glimpse into the nature of jury deliberations in these types of cases and in no way a definitive study of the dynamics of jury deliberations.

Preliminary Data Analysis

The findings from a preliminary examination of the data are consistent with conclusions in the literature that jury deliberations are influenced by a majority effect, in which the pre-deliberation preferences of the individual jurors often predict the eventual post-deliberation verdict. Recall that Table 4-1 shows that in nine of the eleven trials, the first vote revealed a majority (eight majorities in favor of the defense, one in favor of the plaintiff). In each of those cases, the litigant with the first ballot majority eventually prevailed. The other two trials were evenly split 6-6 on the first vote, and in both cases, the jury eventually found for the defense.

The jurors who changed their votes during deliberations were not equally divided among jurors favoring the plaintiff and the defense. Jurors who switched sides during deliberations were much more likely to have initially favored the plaintiff. Of the 20 jurors who changed their votes during deliberations, 17 switched from the plaintiff to the defense, while only three jurors abandoned the defense in favor of the plaintiff.

Bivariate correlations offer an initial look at the relationships between the jurors who changed their votes during deliberations and several other variables of interest. Table 4-3 shows the correlations and their statistical significance. Several factors correlate with a juror changing her vote during deliberations. As discussed above, the literature suggests that as the size of the faction opposed to a juror increases, the probability that the juror will change her position during deliberations should also increase. These data support that finding, with a positive correlation ($r=0.424$, $p<0.01$) between the size of the faction opposed to a juror and that juror changing sides at some point during deliberations.

Non-white jurors appear to be slightly more likely to change positions than white jurors ($r=0.15$, $p<0.05$). And as mentioned above, bivariate correlation confirms that plaintiff jurors were more likely to switch sides than were defense jurors ($r=0.523$, $p<0.01$).

Race was also related to verdict in these trials. Non-white jurors were more likely to find for the plaintiff, which supports the findings of Chapter 2 that white jurors, on average, are more likely to find for the defense in this type of civil lawsuit. While the conclusions of Chapter 2 relied on mock jurors, the results presented here support that finding with verdicts from real jury trials.

Table 4-3: Correlations Between Juror Factors and Deliberation Outcomes

	Foreperson	Female Juror	Non-White Juror	Plaintiff Juror on First Ballot	Juror Changed Sides during Deliberations	Percentage of Jurors Opposed to the Juror on First Ballot
Foreperson	1	-0.192*	-0.088	-0.074	-0.053	-0.090
Female Juror		1	-0.030	0.027	0.057	0.002
Non-White Juror			1	0.171*	0.150*	0.114
Plaintiff Juror on First Ballot				1	0.523**	0.657**
Juror Changed Sides during Deliberations					1	0.424**

Entries are correlations (Pearson's R statistics).
* = Significant at p< 0.05. ** = Significant at p< 0.01.

A negative correlation also appears between female jurors and jurors chosen to be foremen. This means that women, on average, were less likely to be chosen to serve as the jury foreperson. Other studies on jury deliberations have also noticed this tendency (see Vidmar and Hans, 2007, pg. 143). Ellsworth, for example, found that in a study of eighteen mock juries, sixteen chose a male juror to be foreman. In fact, one of the juries in her study was composed of eleven women and one man, and the man was chosen to be foreman (Ellsworth, 1989, pg. 213). Hastie, Schkade and Payne reported similar results. They found that the juror selected to be the foreman was likely to have what the researchers called "dominant" characteristics (Hastie, Schkade and Payne, 1998, pg. 295). That is, the foreperson is more likely to be male and have an above-average level of education (Hans and Vidmar, 1986; Davis, Bray and Holt, 1977 and Strodtbeck and Mann, 1956).

These preliminary bivariate correlations suggest that several characteristics may predispose jurors to change their verdicts during deliberations. Jurors in the minority are more likely to change sides than those in the majority. Jurors who found for the plaintiff seem more likely to switch sides than those who favored the defense. Finally, non-white jurors appear to be more likely to change their votes during deliberations than whites. But which of these factors is most important? A multivariate analysis will estimate the effects of all of these variables on a juror's decision to change sides during deliberations.

A Multivariate Analysis of Jury Deliberations

Table 4-4 presents the results of three models of a juror's decision to change sides during deliberations. In each model, the unit of analysis is the individual juror, and the dependent variable is whether or not the juror changed her vote during deliberations. The decision to change sides is coded as a one if the juror changed her verdict, and a zero if not. Note that only permanent vote changes were coded as a 1. If the juror changed sides at some point but eventually returned to her first-ballot position, the juror was coded as a 0.

Table 4-4: The Determinants of Vote Change During Jury Deliberations

	Model 1	Model 2	Model 3
Juror Voted For Plaintiff at Beginning of Deliberations	2.496* (1.204)	2.462* (1.203)	2.440* (1.112)
Percentage of Jury Opposed to Juror at Beginning of Deliberations	2.201 (2.609)	2.124 (2.530)	2.207 (2.440)
Non-White Juror	–	0.399 (0.477)	0.385 (0.496)
Female Juror	–	–	0.388 (0.630)
Constant	-3.957*** (1.227)	-4.008*** (1.202)	-4.268*** (1.250)
Nagelkerke's R-squared	0.408	0.412	0.417
Sample Size	130	130	130

Dependent Variable is Whether or Not Juror Changed Sides During Deliberations (1 = Changed, 0 = No Change).
Cell entries are logistic regression coefficients, with robust standard errors in parentheses.
* = Significant at p<0.05, ** = Significant at p<0.01, *** = Significant at p<0.001

The independent variables are the juror's race (coded as one for non-white jurors and zero for whites, as the modest sample size does not allow for more specific racial categories), the juror's gender (coded as one for female jurors and zero for males), the jurors verdict at the beginning of deliberations (coded as a one for plaintiff and zero for defense), and the percentage of the jury agreeing with the juror's verdict at the first ballot (ranging from 0 if the juror is the lone dissenter to 1 if the jury is unanimous).

In Model 1, the only explanatory variables are the juror's first-ballot vote at the beginning of deliberations and the percentage of the jury opposed to the juror. Recall that bivariate correlations showed that both of these variables were significantly related to a juror's decision to switch sides during deliberations. When combined in a multivariate model, however, only the juror's verdict preference at the beginning of deliberations remains significantly related to a juror's decision to switch sides. The size of the faction opposed to the juror is still positively correlated with an eventual switch, but the coefficient is not close to statistically-significant levels.

Model 2 adds jurors' race to the model and reveals results very similar to those in Model 1. Again, the only significant predictor of a juror's decision to change her vote during deliberations is the jurors' initial vote for the plaintiff. The size of the opposing faction and the jurors' race, while still positively correlated with an eventual change of vote, are not statistically significant.

Finally, Model 3 adds the juror's gender to the model as an independent variable. The results show that the simultaneous consideration of several potential determinants of a vote change during deliberations leaves only one significant predictor. Those jurors who began deliberations in favor of a plaintiff verdict were more likely to change their votes than were defense jurors, even when the model includes controls for the effects of faction size, juror race and juror gender. Coefficients for juror demographics and faction size are positive, meaning that non-white and female jurors, as well as jurors in a minority faction, may still be more likely to change their votes, but none of these coefficients reach standard levels of statistical significance.

A substantive interpretation of the regression results shows that plaintiff jurors are much more likely to change their votes during deliberations than are defense jurors, but that the overall probability of a juror switching sides, regardless of initial verdict preference, is low. With the values of all of the other variables (race, gender and faction size) held constant at their means, a plaintiff juror has an estimated probability of changing sides during deliberations of 18.1%. This figure, while low, is still very much higher than the estimated probability of 1.9% that a defense juror would eventually switch sides during deliberations.

The finding that a first ballot vote for plaintiff predisposes jurors to change their votes at some point during deliberations is consistent with the "leniency bias" documented in the literature on the effects of jury deliberation. This tendency is not only observed at the level of the juror, but also at the level of the jury. Recall that both of the trials in which deliberations began with the jury evenly split eventually reached a verdict in favor of the defense. However, the findings discussed here are by no means conclusive, as the apparent willingness of plaintiff jurors to change their votes during deliberations may be an artifact of the cases chosen for post-trial interviews, ten out of eleven of which favored the defense.

WHY DO JURORS CHANGE SIDES?

As mentioned above, research on small group decision-making has focused on two mechanisms to explain why jurors, and members of deliberating groups in general, might change their views. The first is a "normative influence" by which group members change views in order to conform to the expectations of others. Under a normative influence, a juror would change her vote after realizing that most of the other members of the jury support the other side. The juror would then feel social pressures to conform to the preferences of the other members of the group. The second mechanism is an "informational influence" under which jurors change their positions after accepting new information from other members of the group.[38] In other words, the process of listening to the perspectives of other jurors may expose the juror to arguments or evidence that the juror had failed to consider. This new information may prompt the juror to change her vote. In their review of the literature on group decision-making, Kaplan and Miller find that "informational influence produces more frequent and stronger shifts than does normative influence," although they concede that, "normative and informational influences operate on group members simultaneously" (Kaplan and Miller, 1987, pg. 306-7).

During the interviews, jurors who switched sides during the deliberations were asked why they changed their votes. The reasons given for these changes fall into two categories. The most common reason given was that jurors changed their minds because other jurors persuaded them with arguments and evidence. Of the 20 jurors who changed their votes at some point during deliberations, 15 reported that they changed because they were convinced by the other jurors that the evidence supported the other side. Jurors who cited this explanation often said that the other jurors had reminded them of a piece of evidence that they had forgotten, or had explained something about the case that the juror had not understood during the trial. These descriptions are consistent with the "information influence" discussed in the small group decision-making literature.

The other reasons given for changing sides had nothing to do with the information jurors heard during deliberations. These jurors typically reported that they were in a small minority faction, and that they felt pressure to vote with the majority in order to give the jury the votes needed to reach a verdict. These jurors clearly felt social pressure to conform to the will of the majority, and eventually acquiesced because they were not sufficiently opposed to a win by the other side to force continued deliberations or a hung jury. During the interviews, the jurors in this category explained that they could not sway the other jurors to agree with their position, and they recognized that further resistance to the majority position was futile. This explanation is somewhat similar to the "normative influence" discussed above, as jurors clearly felt social pressures within the group to conform to a majority position. However, the descriptions these jurors gave of the pressures they felt also referred to the fact that their votes were needed to reach a verdict. Thus, while social pressures may have had some influence on their decision, their vote change may also have been a function of strategic calculations and arguments based on the decision rule. Whichever influence dominated the decision, the effect was relatively modest, as only five of the twenty jurors who changed sides during deliberations reported that their decision was based on factors other than new information.

CONCLUSION

This study offers a brief glimpse into the dynamics of jury deliberations and the factors that influence jurors' decisions to change sides during deliberations. While the data analyzed here are limited, the results are consistent with the "majority effect" described in the literature, in which the pre-deliberation preferences of the jurors often determine the jury's eventual verdict. The results also suggest that the leniency bias observed in other studies of deliberations, particularly in criminal cases, may have also exercised an influence in these civil cases. Jurors' explanations for their vote changes fell into two broad categories described in the literature on the effects of group deliberations. Jurors reported informational and normative effects leading to their vote changes, although the changes that were not attributable to informational effects may have also been affected by strategic dynamics related to the jury's decision rule.

CONCLUSION:

Reforming the Civil Jury

The previous four chapters have examined questions of race and gender in America's civil justice system. After summarizing the findings of these chapters, the book will conclude with a brief discussion of proposed reforms to the civil justice system.

Chapter 1 argued that common methodological problems in studies of juror decision-making have prevented researchers from appreciating the links between jurors' characteristics and their verdicts. Many of these problems, such as the lack of reliable data on civil jury decision-making, are often beyond the control of researchers, as they are the product of limited resources. Other difficulties, however, such as the statistical shortcomings in the literature and an unwillingness to confront strong juror-level effects on verdicts, can and should be corrected.

Chapter 2 presented evidence that juror factors, including race, gender, education, income and attitudes, can affect verdicts in three types of civil litigation. These findings challenged the consensus in the literature that such factors play little if any role in juror decision-making. The results of Chapter 2 also suggest that different people may perceive the "facts" of a case very differently, which reminds us that the civil jury is not simply a fact-finding body, but is also an institution that applies the values and attitudes of the community to the administration of justice.

Chapter 3 argued that the Supreme Court's efforts to end racial discrimination during jury selection have collided with reluctance on the part of the Court to limit the use of the peremptory challenge. The Court's *Batson* decisions have maintained the egalitarian rhetoric seen across a century of jurisprudence combating racial discrimination in jury selection. *Batson* has also created procedural hurdles to blatant race- and gender-discrimination. However, the Court seems to have implicitly recognized that litigants see the peremptory challenge as a necessary tool for seating impartial juries, and has therefore been unwilling to abolish or severely restrict its use. While the intent of the Court's most recent rulings in *Johnson*, *Miller-El* and *Snyder* was clearly to reinvigorate a *Batson* line weakened by *Purkett v. Elem*, the continued existence of the peremptory challenge means that race and gender discrimination during jury selection, while more difficult in theory, remains possible and even likely.

Chapter 4 looked at jury deliberations and explored the factors that may compel jurors to switch sides during deliberations. While most jurors maintain their positions throughout deliberations, some jurors do change their votes. These vote changes are the product of informational, normative and strategic influences. The results of the data analysis also suggest that the "leniency bias" previously documented in criminal trials may also affect civil deliberations.

Tort Reform and the Civil Justice System

Tort reform has become a hot-button political issue. Reform proposals typically call for limits on the monetary damages civil juries can award, changes to liability laws and restrictions on the types of cases juries can hear. Tort reform advocates claim that damages awards have spiraled out of control and that caps are needed to prevent severe damage to the American economy. Indeed, many states have already placed limits on the discretion of the civil jury, and national leaders frequently call for additional tort reform at the federal level. While pundits warn of impending doom brought on by a civil justice system run amok, empirical research continues to find that juries make sound decisions based on the trial evidence. Research on damages awards has also found no evidence of spiraling damages awards or a "litigation crisis" threatening to overwhelm the American economy (Green and Bornstein, 2003).

The debate over tort reform is most often framed as a conflict between trial lawyers on the one side and business corporations on the other. Trial attorneys depict themselves as the defenders of the rights of the injured and wronged, while corporations claim that their resources make them targets of unjustified and frivolous lawsuits. The struggle is thus primarily over money: who has it and who deserves it. But this focus on the financial implications neglects other aspects of the tort reform issue.

Rarely noted in the tort reform debate is that any restrictions on the powers of the civil jury limits democratic participation in the operation of the judiciary. Reforms that limit the discretion of juries place a barrier to the influence of community values and popular will on the administration of justice. Some may argue that such limitations are a positive step, and that members of the general public are ill-equipped to make such decisions. But few would maintain that democratic participation in our system of government should be reduced without careful consideration of the consequences of such a step.

Questions of race and gender have also been largely ignored during the tort reform debate. This book has attempted to show that female and black jurors are more likely to find for the plaintiff in several types of civil litigation. Seen through the prisms of race and gender, tort reform efforts become much more than arguments over economic efficiency. These reform proposals begin to look like an attempt to de-fang one of the very few institutions in which African-Americans, as well as women and the poor, are well represented. Dooley argues that criticisms of the jury reflect fears of an empowered multicultural population (Dooley, 1994-1995). While critics of the civil jury would probably deny that their complaints are motivated at all by issues of race or gender, debates over the civil jury are intimately tied to these political and social cleavages. One can only hope that a more nuanced and thorough debate—a debate that includes a discussion of democratic participation and race, as well as the frequently heard arguments concerning economic productivity and consumer rights—will precede the implementation of any program of comprehensive tort reform.

Endnotes

1. For critics of the American civil jury, see Olson, 1991; Huber, 1991; Drazen, 1989; Huber, 1988; and Austin, 1984.

2. For the methods used by individual states to summon prospective jurors for duty, see Starr and McCormick, 2001, pp. 41-2. For more on the changes in jury selection systems that have occurred in recent decades, see Van Dyke, 1977.

3. Kalven and Zeisel point out that the 79% agreement rate between judges and juries compares very favorably to individuals asked to judge complex questions in other areas, such as doctors asked to diagnose a patient (77% agreement) and NSF reviewers determining which projects to fund (75% agreement).

4. For some of the many studies that have found no relationship between jurors' personal characteristics and their verdicts, see Diamond, 2006; Eisenberg and Wells, 2002; Saks, 2002; Devine, et al., 2001; Saks, 1997; Hastie, 1991; Visher, 1987; Hepburn, 1980; Berk, Hennesey and Swan, 1977; Davis, Bray and Holt, 1977 and Saks, 1976.

5. For more on the story model, see Pennington and Hastie, 1993; Pennington and Hastie, 1992; Pennington and Hastie, 1991 and Pennington and Hastie, 1986. A history of the story model's development appears in Vidmar and Hans, 2007, pp. 132-5.

6. "Ten Years After Simpson Verdict: Issue of Race Still Figures Prominently in Public Opinion," NBC News Poll, reported June 6, 2004. After Simpson's civil trial, another

poll revealed that, "whites overwhelmingly agreed with the jury's decision that Simpson is responsible for the deaths of Nicole Brown Simpson and Ronald Goldman. Only about a fourth of blacks agreed with the verdict." "Race Factor Tilts the Scale of Public Opinion," USA Today, February 5, 1997.

7. These findings are similar to those reported in Foley and Chamblin, 1982. For a review of other studies on the effects of race in racially-charged criminal trials, see King, 1993.

8. Denove and Imwinklereid's scenario is a bit silly, as it is hard to imagine suing a friend because you got sick at his backyard barbeque. However, the experiment does demonstrate that the identity of the defendant affects jurors' views of a case.

9. As part of an evaluation of recent jury reforms in Arizona, the Arizona Supreme Court allowed researchers to videotape the deliberations of several trials conducted between 1998 and 2001. Data from those recordings have been used in several articles, including Diamond, Rose and Murphy, 2006.

10. Visher concedes that there are problems inherent in interviewing jurors after deliberation, "it is possible that jurors' recollections of their pre-deliberation guilt judgments were influenced by the deliberation process. No solution exists for this problem" (Visher, 1987, pg. 8, footnote 6)

11. In her study 1987, Visher tries to get around this problem by only interviewing jurors who served on sexual assault trials, and by recording certain aspects of the case, such as certain types of evidence and some of the victim's characteristics.

12. See, for example, Hastie, Schkade and Payne, 1998, (N=726 from Denver, CO area); Bornstein and Rajki, 1994, (N=237 from Baton Rouge, LA) or Denove and Imwinkelreid, 1995, (N=400 from Sacramento and Los Angeles, CA).

13. Studies that make use of "convenience samples" include Sommers and Ellsworth, 2000, (subjects approached in an

international airport terminal); Bornstein and Rajki, 1994, (subjects approached outside a department store) and Denove and Imwinkelreid, 1995, (sample described only as "convenience sample," collected from people at a shopping mall, park or bowling alley.)

14. For a review of methodological concerns in mock trial research, see Breau and Brook, 2007.

15. Breau and Brook (2007) found that "consequentiality" – that is, the fact that a group knows that its decision makes no real difference – affected the outcome of small-group decisions. Their findings are based on a very small group of student jurors deciding a hypothetical law school honor code violation, but the results raise interesting questions for further research.

16. For the benefits of active role playing in social science experiments, see Krupat, 1977, pg. 501.

17. Eisenberg and Wells' 2002 study makes use of the state and federal court data sets.

18. Helland and Tabarrok's 2003 study relies primarily on the JVR data, but also makes some use of the data from the state and federal courts.

19. For more on the comparative merits of different methods in studies of juror decision-making, see Sommers and Ellsworth, 2003 and MacCoun, 1993.

20. Most recent studies use multivariate models to control for the effects of different demographic factors. But for older studies that rely solely on bivariate measures, see Hepburn, 1980; Bernard, 1979 and Green, 1968.

21. For studies reporting low R-squared statistics in demographic models of juror decision-making, see, for example, Saks, 1997; Visher, 1987 and Hastie, Penrod and Pennington, 1983

22. For additional studies commenting on the disproportionate scholarly attention on criminal jury behavior, see Devine, et al., 2001; Diamond, Saks and Landsmann, 1999 and Hastie, Penrod and Pennington, 1983.

23. Diamond and Saks have both written on the lack of any relationship between jury verdicts and the personal characteristics of the jurors. See, for example, Diamond, 1990; Saks, 2002 and Saks, 1997.

24. Throughout this chapter, I will refer to "civil litigation," "civil cases," or "civil lawsuits." With these terms, I am referring to tort cases, which are a subset of all civil litigation. There are many other types of civil procedure, including equity claims (where the remedy sought is some form of court order, such as an injunction), bankruptcy, divorce, and so on. But the focus here, as in most other studies of juror decision-making in civil trials, will be on tort cases in the common law tradition, in which a plaintiff seeks money damages to remedy an injury allegedly caused by the defendant.

25. Verdicts seldom, if ever, differ as a result of the presentation format. In other words, the same case presented by an attorney on videotape will yield the same, or at least a very similar, verdict when presented live.

26. The finding that Asian-American jurors were the more likely to find for the defense in these cases should be taken with a certain amount of caution. Asian-Americans participated in significant numbers in only a few of the mock trials (see Appendix A) and the apparent effects of race may in fact be nothing more than the impact of factors unique to those particular cases.

27. These cases involve the systematic exclusion of African-Americans and Latinos from the lists used to select prospective members of grand juries and jury venires. See *Strauder v. West Virginia* 100 U.S. 303 (1879), *Ex parte Virginia* 100 U.S. 330 (1879), *Neal v. Delaware* 103 U.S.

370 (1880), *Bush v. Kentucky* 107 U.S. 110 (1883), *Carter v. Texas* 177 U.S. 442 (1900), *Rogers v. Alabama* 192 U.S. 226 (1904), *Norris v. Alabama* 394 U.S. 587 (1935), *Hollins v. Oklahoma* 295 U.S. 394 (1935), *Hale v. Kentucky* 303 U.S. 316 (1938), *Smith v. Texas* 311 U.S. 128 (1941), *Hill v. Texas* 316 U.S. 400 (1942), *Patton v. Mississippi* 332 U.S. 463 (1947), *Cassel v. Texas* 339 U.S. 282 (1950), *Avery v. Georgia* 345 U.S. 559 (1953), *Reese v. Georgia* 350 U.S. 57 (1955), *Eubanks v. Louisiana* 356 U.S. 584 (1958), *Arnold v. North Carolina* 376 U.S. 773 (1964), *Whitus v. Georgia* 385 U.S. 545 (1967), *Jones v. Georgia* 389 U.S. 24 (1967), *Sims v. Georgia* 389 U.S. 404 (1967), *Turner v. Fouche* 396 U.S. 346 (1970), *Alexander v. Louisiana* 405 U.S. 625 (1972), *Peters v. Kiff* 407 U.S. 493 (1972), *Castaneda v. Partida* 430 U.S. 482 (1977), *Rose v. Mitchell* 443 U.S. 545 (1979) and *Vasquez v. Hillery* 474 U.S. 254 (1986).

28. Also of note in the *Swain* decision is the Court's definition of "impartial," which differs from the definition found in earlier anti-discrimination and "fair cross-section" cases. In Swain, an impartial jury is one in which the litigants have had the unrestricted use of their peremptory challenges to eliminate from the panel any jurors the litigants view as favoring the opposition. The jurors remaining after each side has used its peremptories are impartial. Contrast that with the language of the *Strauder* line and "fair cross-section" cases, in which a jury is impartial if women and racial minorities have not been systematically excluded. In these cases, only a jury that reflects the views and values of the entire community can be seen as "impartial." While the *Swain* Court saw the impartial jury from the perspective of excluding partiality, the "fair cross-section" cases view an impartial jury as one that does not exclude the diversity of views brought about by a representative jury.

29. While the effect of the *Batson* decision was to make race-based peremptory challenges illegal, the fundamental difference between *Batson* and *Swain* was in fact a change in

the burden of proof needed to show racial discrimination. In *Swain*, the Court held that evidence of discrimination across numerous cases was needed to challenge a prosecutor's peremptories. In *Batson*, the Court ruled that proof of discrimination in a single jury selection was sufficient to warrant a remedy.

30. Although the Court's decision was based on the Fourteenth Amendment's Equal Protection Clause, *Batson* was argued on Sixth Amendment grounds. Mr. Batson's attorneys argued that race-based peremptories violated his right to an impartial jury. The Court majority, while finding for the appellant, rejected this argument and instead based its decision on a theory that race-based peremptories violated the Equal Protection rights of the defendant as well as the improperly excluded jurors.

31. Prima facie is Latin for "on its first appearance" or "on its face" and means that, at first glance, the evidence presented establishes a fact. However, that evidence can still be rebutted. Under Batson, the objecting attorney must show a prima facie case of the discriminatory use of peremptory challenges.

32. Courts in some states (including California) have refused to follow *Purkett*, and have ruled instead that their State Constitutions require persuasive neutral explanations for challenged peremptory strikes (see Brown, 1998-1999, pp. 407-8).

33. For arguments in favor of abolishing the peremptory challenge, see Broderick, 1992; Alschuler, 1989; Purtell, 1988-1989 and Justice Marshall's opinion in *Batson v. Kentucky* 476 U.S. 79 (1986), (J. Marshall, concurring) at 103. The popular media has also begun to weigh in on the peremptory challenge. The *Los Angeles Times* has suggested that the time to abolish the peremptory may be at hand (see *Los Angeles Times*, "Judging juries," April 20, 2006, pg. B12).

34. Diamond *et al.* point out that using first ballot votes may be problematic, because deliberations may not begin with a vote but with a discussion of the case instead. This discussion may influence juror's verdict preferences, thereby bringing the first ballot vote closer to the eventual verdict (see Diamond, Rose and Murphy, 2006).

35. Most civil verdicts do not require a unanimous verdict, although unanimity is required in civil cases in federal courts. While the decision rule varies from state to state, a super-majority of 9 - 3 or 10 - 2 is typical. For the decision rules in the individual states, see Starr and McCormick, 2001.

36. Jurors in the minority during deliberations may also have a reduced effect on the verdict because unanimity is not required in most civil trials. For more on deliberations in non-unanimous civil juries, see Diamond, Rose and Murphy, 2006.

37. For descriptions of the seriousness with which mock jurors approach their verdict decisions, see Priest, 2002, pg. vii and Krupat, 1977, pg. 501.

38. For more on these two types of social influence and their effects on group decision making, see Zuber, Crott and Werner, 1992; Kaplan and Miller, 1987 and Isenberg, 1986.

References

Alexander v. Louisiana 405 U.S. 625 (1972).

Allen v. Hardy 478 U.S. 255 (1986).

Alschuler, Albert W., 1989, "The Supreme Court and the Jury: Voir Dire, Peremptory Challenges and the Review of Jury Verdicts," 56 *University of Chicago Law Review* 153.

Arnold v. North Carolina 376 U.S. 773 (1964).

Austin, Arthur D., 1984, *Complex Litigation Confronts the Jury System: A Case Study*, University Publications of America, Frederick, Maryland.

Avery v. Georgia 345 U.S. 559 (1953).

Babcock, Barbara, 1975, "Voir Dire: Preserving 'Its Wonderful Power,'" 27 *Stanford Law Review* 545.

Bailis, Daniel S. and Robert J. MacCoun, 1996, "Estimating Liability Risks with the Media as Your Guide," 20 *Law and Human Behavior* 419.

Ballard v. U.S. 329 U.S. 187 (1946).

Batson v. Kentucky 476 U.S. 79 (1986).

Berk, Richard A., Michael Hennesey and James Swan, 1977, "The Vagaries and Vulgarities of 'Scientific' Jury Selection," 1 *Evaluation Quarterly* 143.

Bernard, J. L., 1979, "Interaction Between the Race of the Defendant and That of Jurors in Determining Verdicts," 5 *Law and Psychology* Review 103.

Bonazzoli, M. Juliet, 1998, "Jury Selection and Bias: Debunking Invidious Stereotypes Through Science," 18 *Quinnipiac Law Review* 247.

Bornstein, Brian H. and Michelle Rajki, 1994, "Extra-legal Factors and Product Liability: The Influence of Mock Jurors' Demographic Characteristics and Intuitions about the Cause of an Injury," 12 *Behavioral Science and the Law* 127.

Bowers, William J., Benjamin D. Steiner and Marla Sandys, 2001, "Death Sentencing in Black and White: An Empirical Analysis of the Role of Jurors' Race and Jury Racial Composition," 3 *University of Pennsylvania Journal of Constitutional Law* 171.

Boyll, Jeffery, R., 1991, "Psychological, Cognitive, Personality and Interpersonal Factors in Jury Verdicts," 15 *Law and Psychology Review* 163.

Bray, Karen M., 1992, "Comment: Reaching the Final Chapter in the Story of Peremptory Challenges," 40 *UCLA Law Review* 517.

Bray, Robert M. and Norbert L. Kerr, 1982, "Methodological Considerations in the Study of the Psychology of the Courtroom, " in Norbert l. Kerr and Robert M. Bray (eds.) *The Psychology of the Courtroom*, Academic Press, New York.

Breau, David L. and Brian Brook, 2007, "'Mock' Mock Juries: A Field Experiment on the Ecological Validity of Jury Simulations," 31 *Law and Psychology Review* 77.

Broderick, Raymond J., 1992, "Why the Peremptory Challenge Should Be Abolished," 65 *Temple Law Review* 369.

Brown, Cheryl A. C., 1998-1999, "Challenging the Challenge: Twelve Years after *Batson*, Courts are still Struggling to Fill in the Gaps left by the Supreme Court," 28 *University of Baltimore Law Review* 379.

Bush v. Kentucky 107 U.S. 110 (1883).

Carter v. Texas 177 U.S. 442 (1900).

Cassel v. Texas 339 U.S. 282 (1950).

Castaneda v. Partida 430 U.S. 482 (1977).

Cavise, Leonard L., 1999, "The *Batson* Doctrine: The Supreme Court's Utter Failure to Meet the Challenge of Discrimination in Jury Selection," 1999 *Wisconsin Law Review* 501.

Chapman, Nathan Seth, 2006, "Punishment by the People: Rethinking the Jury's Political role in Assigning Punitive Damages," 56 *Duke Law Journal* 1119.

Charlow, Robin, 1997-1998, "Tolerating Deception and Discrimination after *Batson*," 50 *Stanford Law Review* 9.

Constable, Marianne, 1994, *The Law of the Other: The Mixed Jury and Changing Conceptions of Citizenship, Law and Knowledge*, The University of Chicago Press, Chicago and London.

Cressler, Michael A., 1992, "Comment: *Powers v. Ohio*, the Death Knell for the Peremptory Challenge?" 28 *Idaho Law Review* 349.

Davis, James H., Mark Stasson, Kaoru Ono and Suzi Zimmerman, 1988, "Effects of Straw Polls on Group Decision Making: Sequential Voting Pattern, Timing, and Local Majorities," 55 *Journal of Personality and Social Psychology* 918.

Davis, James H., Robert M. Bray and Robert W. Holt, 1977, "The Empirical Study of Decision Processes in Juries: A Critical Review" in June Louin Tapp and Felice J. Levine (eds.) *Law, Justice and the Individual in Society: Psychological and Legal Issues*, Holt, Rinehart and Winston Publishers, New York, New York.

Denove, Chris F. and Edward J. Imwinkelreid, 1995, "Jury Selection: An Empirical Investigation of Demographic Bias," 19 *American Journal of Trial Advocacy* 285.

Devine, Dennis J., Laura D. Clayton, Benjamin B. Dunford, Rasmy Seying, and Jennifer Pryce, 2001, "Jury Decision Making: 45 Years of Empirical Research on Deliberating Groups," 7 *Psychology, Public Policy and Law* 622.

Diamond, Shari Seidman, 2006, "Beyond Fantasy and Nightmare: A Portrait of the Jury," 54 *Buffalo Law Review* 717.

Diamond, Shari Seidman, Mary R. Rose and Beth Murphy, 2006, "Revisiting the Unanimity Requirement: The Behavior of the Non-Unanimous Civil Jury," 100 *Northwestern University Law Review* 201.

Diamond, Shari Seidman, Michael J. Saks and Stephen Landsmann, 1999, "Juror Judgments about Liability and Damages: Sources of Variability and Ways to Increase Consistency," 48 *DePaul Law Review* 301.

Diamond, Shari Seidman, Leslie Ellis and Elisabeth Schmidt, 1997-1998, "Realistic Responses to the Limitations of *Batson v. Kentucky*," 7 *Cornell Journal of Law and Public Policy* 77.

Diamond, Shari, 1990, "Scientific Jury Selection: What Social Scientists Know and Do Not Know," 73 *Judicature* 178.

Dooley, Laura Gaston, 1994-1995, "Our Juries, Our Selves: The Power, Perception and Politics of the Civil Jury," 80 *Cornell Law Review* 325.

Drazen, Dan, 1989, "The Case for Special Juries in Toxic Tort Litigation," 72 *Judicature* 292.

Edmonson v. Leesville Concrete Company 500 U. S. 614 (1991).

Eisenberg, Theodore and Martin T. Wells, 2002, "Trial Outcomes and Demographics: Is there a 'Bronx Effect'?" 80 *Texas Law Review* 1839.

Ellsworth, Phoebe C., 1989, "Are Twelve Heads Better Than One?" 52 *Law and Contemporary Problems* 205.

Eubanks v. Louisiana 356 U.S. 584 (1958).

Ex parte Virginia 100 U.S. 330 (1879).

Feild, H. and N. Barnett, 1978, "Simulating Jury Trials: Students vs. 'Real' People as Jurors," 104 *Journal of Social Psychology* 287.

Foley, Linda A. and Minor H. Chamblin, 1982, "The Effect of Race and Personality on Mock Jurors' Decisions," 112 *The Journal of Psychology* 47.

Fowler, Lucy, 2005, "Gender and Jury Deliberations: The Contributions of Social Science," 12 *William and Mary Journal of Women and Law* 1.

Galanter, Marc, 1993, "The Regulatory Function of the Civil Jury," in Litan, Robert E. (ed.), *Verdict: Assessing the Civil Jury System*, The Brookings Institution, Washington, DC.

Garber, Steven and Anthony G. Bower, 1999, "Newspaper Coverage of Automotive Product Liability Verdicts," 33 *Law and Society Review* 93.

Georgia v. McCollum 505 U.S. 42 (1992).

Green, Edward, 1968, "The Reasonable Man: Legal Fiction or Psychosocial Reality?" 2 *Law and Society Review* 241.

Greene, Edie and Brian H. Bornstein, 2003, Determining Damages: The Psychology of Jury Awards, American Psychological Association, Washington, DC.

Haddon, Phoebe A., 1994, "Rethinking the Jury," 3 *William and Mary Bill of Rights Journal* 29.

Hale v. Kentucky 303 U.S. 316 (1938).

Hans, Valerie, P., 2000, *Business on Trial: The Civil Jury and Corporate Responsibility*, Yale University Press, New Haven and London.

Hans, Valerie and M. David Ermann, 1989, "Responses to Corporate Versus Individual Wrong-Doing," 13 *Law and Human Behavior* 151.

Hans, Valerie P. and Neil Vidmar, 1986, *Judging the Jury*, Plenum Press, New York and London.

Hastie, Reid, David A. Schkade and John W. Payne, 1998, "A Study of Juror and Jury Judgments in Civil Cases: Deciding Liability for Punitive Damages," 22 *Law and Human Behavior* 287.

Hastie, Reid, 1991, "Is Attorney-Conducted Voir Dire an Effective Procedure for the Selection of Impartial Juries?" 40 *The American University Law Review* 703.

Hastie, Reid, Steven D. Penrod and Nancy Pennington, 1983, *Inside the Jury*, Harvard University Press, Cambridge, Massachusetts and London, England.

Helland, Eric and Alexander Tabarrok, 2003, "Race, Poverty and American Tort Awards: Evidence from Three Data Sets," 32 *The Journal of Legal Studies* 27.

Hepburn, John R., 1980, "The Objective Reality of Evidence and the Utility of Systematic Jury Selection," 4 *Law and Human Behavior* 89.

Hernandez v. New York 500 U.S. 352 (1991).

Hill v. Texas 316 U.S. 400 (1942).

Hollins v. Oklahoma 295 U.S. 394 (1935).

Howard, Judith A. and B. Douglas Leber, 1988, "Socializing Attribution: Generalizations to 'Real' Social Environments," 88 *Journal of Applied Social Psychology* 664.

Hoyt v. Florida 368 U.S. 57 (1961).

Huber, Peter, 1991, *Galileo's Revenge: Junk Science in the Courtroom*, Basic Books, New York.

Huber, Peter, 1988, *Liability: The Legal Revolution and its Consequences*, Basic Books, New York.

Isenberg, Daniel J., 1986, "Group Polarization: A Critical Review and Meta-Analysis," 50 *Journal of Personality and Social Psychology* 1141.

J.E.B. v. Alabama 511 U.S. 127 (1994).

Johnson v. California 545 U.S. ___ Docket No. 04-6964 (2005).

Jonakait, Randolph N., 2003, *The American Jury System*, Yale University Press, New Haven and London.

Jones v. Georgia 389 U.S. 24 (1967).

Kalven, Harry and Hans Zeisel, 1966, *The American Jury*, Little, Brown and Company, Boston and Toronto.

Kaplan, Martin F. and Charles E. Miller, 1987, "Group Decision Making and Normative Versus Informational Influence: Effects of Type of Issue and Assigned Decision Rule," 53 *Journal of Personality and Social Psychology* 306.

Kerr, Norbert L and Robert J, MacCoun, 1985, "The Effects of Jury Size and Polling Method on the Process and Product of Jury Deliberations," 48 *Journal of Personality and Social Psychology* 349.

King, Nancy, 1993, "Post-conviction Review of Jury Discrimination: Measuring the Effects of Juror Race on Jury Decisions," 92 *Michigan Law Review* 63.

Krupat, E., 1977, "A Re-Assessment of Role Playing as a Technique in Social Psychology," 3 *Personality and Social Psychology Bulletin* 498.

Landsman, Stephan, 1993, "The History and Objectives of the Civil Jury System," in Robert E. Litan (ed.), *Verdict: Assessing the Civil Jury System*, The Brookings Institution, Washington, D.C.

Leach, Brian E., 1994-1995, "Extending *Batson v. Kentucky* to Gender and Beyond: The Death Knell for the Peremptory Challenge," 19 *Southern Illinois University Law Journal* 381.

Liebeck v. McDonald's (1994).

Los Angeles Times, "Judging juries," April 20, 2006.

MacCoun, Robert, 1993, "Inside the Black Box: What Empirical Research Tells Us about Decision-Making by Civil Juries," in Robert E. Litan (ed.), *Verdict: Assessing the Civil Jury System*, The Brookings Institution, Washington, D.C.

MacCoun, Robert J. and Norbert L. Kerr, 1988, "Asymmetric Influence in Mock Jury Deliberations: Jurors' Bias for Leniency," 54 *Journal of Personality and Social Psychology* 21.

Marder, Nancy S., 2006, "Justice Stevens, The Peremptory Challenge, and the Jury," 74 *Fordham Law Review* 1683.

Miller, Marina and Jay Hewitt, 1978, "Conviction of a Defendant as a Function of a Juror-Victim Racial Similarity," 105 *Journal of Social Psychology* 159.

Miller-El v. Dretke 545 U.S. ___ Docket No. 03-9659 (2005).

Mililli, Kenneth J., 1996, "*Batson* in Practice: What We Have Learned About *Batson* and Peremptory Challenges," 71 *Notre Dame Law Review* 447.

Missouri v. Antwine 743 S.W. 2d 51 (1987).

Muller, Eric L., 1997, "Solving the *Batson* Paradox: Harmless Error, Jury Representation and the Sixth Amendment," 106 *Yale Law Journal* 93.

Nagel, Stuart and Lenore Weitzman, 1972, "Sex and the Unbiased Jury," 56 *Judicature* 108.

Naranjo v. Toyota Motor Company, Bexar County, Texas, Cause No. 2000-C116451, 2005.

NBC News Poll, reported June 6, 2004, "Ten Years After Simpson Verdict: Issue of Race Still Figures Prominently in Public Opinion."

Neal v. Delaware 103 U.S. 370 (1880).

Norris v. Alabama 394 U.S. 587 (1935).

Olson, Walter K., 1991, *The Litigation Explosion: What Happened When America Unleashed the Lawsuit*, Truman Talley Books-Dutton, New York.

Page, Anthony, 2005, "*Batson's* Blind Spot: Unconscious Stereotyping and the Peremptory Challenge," 85 *Boston University Law Review* 155.

Patton v. Mississippi 332 U.S. 463 (1947).

Pennington, Nancy and Reid Hastie, 1993, "The Story Model for Juror Decision-Making," in *Inside the Juror: The Psychology of Juror Decision Making*, Hastie, Reid (ed.), Cambridge University Press, Cambridge, Massachusetts.

Pennington, Nancy and Reid Hastie, 1992, "Explaining the Evidence: Tests of the Story Model for Juror Decision-Making," 62 *Journal of Personality and Social Psychology* 189.

Pennington, Nancy and Reid Hastie, 1991, "A Cognitive Theory of Juror Decision-Making: The Story Model," 13 *Cordoza Law Review* 519.

Pennington, Nancy and Reid Hastie, 1986, "Evidence Evaluation in Complex Decision-Making," 51 *Journal of Personality and Social Psychology* 242.

Peters v. Kiff 407 U.S. 493 (1972).

Pizzi, William T.,1987, "*Batson v. Kentucky*: Curing the Disease but Killing the Patient," *Supreme Court Review* 97.

Powers v. Ohio 499 U.S. 400 (1992).

Priest, George, L., 2002, "Preface and Acknowledgments" in Cass R. Sunstein, Reid Hastie, John W. Payne, David A. Schkade and W. Kip Viscusi (eds.), *Punitive Damages: How Juries Decide*, University of Chicago Press, Chicago and London.

Priest, George L. and Benjamin Klein, 1984, "The Selection of Disputes for Litigation," 13 *Journal of Legal Studies* 1.

Purkett v. Elem 514 U.S. 765 (1995).

Purtell, Rosemary, 1988-1989, "The Continued Use of Discriminatory Peremptory Challenges after *Batson v. Kentucky*: Is the Only Alternative to Eliminate the Peremptory Challenge Itself?" 23 *New England Law Review* 221.

Raphael, Michael J. and Edward J. Ungvarsky, 1994, "Excuses, Excuses: Neutral Explanations under *Batson v. Kentucky*," 27 *University of Michigan Journal of Legal Reform* 229.

Reese v. Georgia 350 U.S. 57 (1955).

Robbennolt, Jennifer K., 2005, "Evaluating Juries by Comparison to Judges: A Benchmark for Judging?" 32 *Florida State University Law Review* 469.

Rogers v. Alabama 192 U.S. 226 (1904).

Rose, Mary R. and Neil Vidmar, 2002, "The Bronx 'Bronx Jury': A Profile of Civil Jury Awards in New York Counties" 80 *Texas Law Review* 1887.

Rose v. Mitchell 443 U.S. 545 (1979).

Saks, Michael, J., 2002, "Trial Outcomes and Demographics: Easy Assumptions versus Hard Evidence," 80 *Texas Law Review* 1877.

Saks, Michael, J., 1997, "What Do Jury Experiments Tell Us About How Juries (Should) Make Decisions?" 6 *Southern California Interdisciplinary Law Journal* 40.

Saks, Michael J., 1976, "The Limits of Scientific Jury Selection: Ethical and Empirical," 17 *Jurimetrics Journal* 3.

Sandys, Marla and Ronald C. Dillehay, 1995, "First-Ballot Votes, Predeliberation Dispositions, and Final Verdicts in Jury Trials," 19 *Law and Human Behavior* 175.

Schkade, David A., Cass R. Sunstein and Daniel Kahneman, 2002, "Deliberating About Dollars: The Severity Shift," in Cass R. Sunstein, Reid Hastie, John W. Payne, David A. Schkade and W. Kip Viscusi (eds.), *Punitive Damages: How Juries Decide*, University of Chicago Press, Chicago and London.

Schwarzer, William W. and Alan Hirsch, 1993, "The Modern American Jury: Reflections on Veneration and Distrust," in Robert E. Litan (ed.) *Verdict: Assessing the Civil Jury System*, The Brookings Institution, Washington, D.C.

Sears, David O., 1985, "College Sophomores in the Laboratory: Influences of a Narrow Data Base on Social Psychology's View of Human Nature," 51 *Journal of Personality and Social Psychology* 515.

Sims v. Georgia 389 U.S. 404 (1967).

Sommers, Samuel R., 2006, "On Racial Diversity and Group Decision-Making: Identifying Multiple Effects of Racial Composition on Jury Deliberations," *Journal of Personality and Social Psychology* (in print).

Sommers, Samuel R. and Phoebe C. Ellsworth, 2003, "How Much Do We Really Know About Race and Juries?: A Review of Social Science Theory and Research," 78 *Chicago-Kent Law Review* 997.

Sommers, Samuel R. and Phoebe C. Ellsworth, 2000, "Race in the Courtroom: Perceptions of Guilt and Dispositional Attributions," 26 *Personality and Social Psychology Bulletin* 1367.

Smith v. Texas 311 U.S. 128 (1941).

Snyder v. Louisiana 552 U.S. ___ No. 06-10119 (2008).

Starr, Hale V. and Mark McCormick, 2001, *Jury Selection*, Third Edition, Aspen Law and Business Publishers.

Stoltz, Brian W., 2006, "Rethinking the Peremptory Challenge: Letting Lawyers Enforce the Principles of *Batson*," 85 *Texas Law Review* 1031.

Strauder v. West Virginia 100 U.S. 303 (1879).

Strodtbeck, Fred L. and Richard D. Mann, 1956, "Sex Role Differentiation in Jury Deliberations," 19 *Sociometry* 3.

Swain v. Alabama 380 U.S. 202 (1965).

Sward, Ellen E., 2001, *The Decline of the Civil Jury*, Carolina Academic Press, Durham, North Carolina.

Swift, Joshua E., 1992-1993, "*Batson*'s Invidious Legacy: Discriminatory Juror Exclusion and the Intuitive Peremptory Challenge," 78 *Cornell Law Review* 336.

Taylor v. Louisiana 419 U.S. 522 (1975).

Tindale, R. Scott, James H. Davis, David A. Vollrath and Dennis H. Nagao, 1990, "Asymmetrical Social Influence in Freely Interacting Groups: A Test of Three Models," 58 *Journal of Personality and Social Psychology* 438.

Turner v. Fouche 396 U.S. 346 (1970).

Underwood, Barbara D., 1992, "Ending Race Discrimination in Jury Selection: Whose Right Is It, Anyway?" 92 *Columbia Law Review* 725.

USA Today, "Race Factor Tilts the Scale of Public Opinion," February 5, 1997.

Van Dyke, Jon M., 1977, *Jury Selection Procedures: Our Uncertain Commitment to Representative Juries*, Ballinger Publishing Company, Cambridge, Massachusetts.

Vasquez v. Hillery 474 U.S. 254 (1986).

Vidmar, Neil and Valerie Hans, 2007, *American Juries: The Verdict*, Prometheus Books, Amherst, New York.

Visher, Christy A., 1987, "Juror Decision Making: The Importance of Evidence," 11 *Law and Human Behavior* 1.

Waldfogel, Joel, 1995, "The Selection Hypothesis and the Relationship between Trial and Plaintiff Victory," 103 *Journal of Political Economy* 229.

Weiten, W. and Sheri Diamond, 1979, "A Critical Review of the Jury Simulation Paradigm: The Case of Defendant Characteristics," 3 *Law and Human Behavior* 71.

Wissler, Roselle L., Allen J. Hart and Michael J. Saks, 2000, "Decisionmaking About General Damages: A Comparison of Jurors, Judges and Lawyers," 98 *Michigan Law Review* 751.

Whitus v. Georgia 385 U.S. 545 (1967).

Zuber, Johannes A., Helmut W. Crott and Joachim Werner, 1992, "Choice Shift and Group Polarization: An Analysis of the Status of Arguments and Social Decision Schemes," 62 *Journal of Personality and Social Psychology* 50.

APPENDIX A:

Description of Mock Trial Samples

	N	Demographics			
		Female	Black	Latino	Asian
Car Accident Trials					
Sacramento, CA	224	50.9%	15.6%	19.6%	13.8%
Macon, GA	320	54.5%	82.1%	0.0%	0.9%
Lincolnwood, IL	216	52.3%	16.8%	16.8%	10.7%
Indianapolis, IN	67	47.8%	25.4%	0.0%	0.0%
Port Gibson, MS	142	54.9%	76.3%	0.0%	0.0%
Libby, MT	128	51.6%	0.8%	0.0%	0.0%
Houston, TX	208	49.5%	24.3%	24.6%	0.0%
Marshall, TX	195	51.3%	47.7%	1.0%	0.0%
TOTAL	**1,500**	**52.0%**	**40.2%**	**8.9%**	**3.8%**
Prescription Drug Trials					
Bethesda, MD	59	49.2%	35.6%	8.5%	0.0%
Dallas-Fort Worth, TX (x2)	409	51.0%	21.8%	19.3%	0.1%
Laredo, TX	268	52.2%	1.5%	83.1%	0.4%
Russellville, AR	195	59.3%	19.6%	0.0%	1.0%
Houston, TX	195	60.8%	24.6%	25.1%	0.0%
Union County, NJ	308	60.4%	33.9%	6.2%	2.0%
Riverside, CA	817	51.4%	16.2%	26.8%	17.5%
Charleston, WV	194	65.5%	1.0%	1.0%	0.0%
Middlesex County, MA	210	53.1%	5.3%	4.3%	5.3%
TOTAL	**2,655**	**54.8%**	**17.0%**	**22.8%**	**6.3%**

		Demographics			
	N	Female	Black	Latino	Asian
Accounting Trials					
Columbus, OH	224	50.0%	30.5%	0.9%	0.4%
Portland, OR	89	52.8%	7.9%	1.1%	9.0%
Spokane, WA	93	53.8%	1.1%	3.2%	1.1%
Garden Grove, CA	54	53.7%	5.6%	22.2%	14.8%
Tucson, AZ	99	51.0%	0.8%	35.9%	0.8%
Phoenix, AZ (x3)	508	53.9%	15.2%	13.3%	0.6%
San Francisco, CA (x2)	528	49.5%	18.4%	16.5%	23.4%
Dallas, TX	39	46.2%	23.1%	12.8%	0.0%
New York, NY	251	50.8%	19.0%	23.2%	12.5%
Pittsburgh, PA	43	51.2%	18.6%	0.0%	0.0%
Winston-Salem, NC	28	56.1%	25.6%	8.5%	0.0%
Anaheim, CA	57	48.2%	5.4%	17.9%	16.1%
Milwaukee, WI	39	59.0%	17.9%	15.4%	0.0%
Newark, NJ	216	54.4%	31.3%	5.5%	3.2%
Cincinnati, OH	38	50.0%	21.1%	0.0%	0.0%
Los Angeles, CA	144	50.5%	18.4%	35.9%	10.7%
Boston, MA	59	47.5%	13.6%	8.6%	3.4%
TOTAL	**2,509**	**51.6%**	**17.1%**	**15.1%**	**7.9%**

APPENDIX B:

Demographic and Attitudinal Variables

***Question Wording* and Coding** (all variables have bee re-coded to range between 0 and 1)
Sex: Male = 0, Female = 1

Please classify your ethnic background: Re-coded into dummy variables for African-Americans, Latinos, Asian-Americans and Whites.

Your age in years: (Re-scaled to range between 0 and 1.)

Your highest level of education: No High School diploma = 1, High School Diploma/GED only = 2, Technical School = 3, Jr. College or Some College = 4, College Degree = 5, Graduate Degree = 6.

Your total yearly family income: $15,000 or less = 1, $15,000-$25,000 = 2, $25,000-$35,000 = 3, $35,000-$50,000 = 4, $50,000-$75,000 = 5, $75,000 or more = 6.

Politically you are: Liberal = -1, Middle of the road = 0, Conservative = 1.

Business Regulation Index (Respondent's answers to the following five questions are summed and then re-scaled to range between 0 and 1.)[a]

I really don't trust big business. Disagree = -2, Somewhat disagree = -1, Somewhat Agree = 1, Agree = 2, Missing Value = 0.

Most corporations "cook their books" and report false information to the public. Disagree = -2, Somewhat disagree = -1, Somewhat Agree = 1, Agree = 2, Missing Value = 0.

Government regulators, who are supposed to oversee corporations, often put the good of the corporation above the good of the public. Disagree = -2, Somewhat disagree = -1, Somewhat Agree = 1, Agree = 2, Missing Value = 0.

Do you think big companies try to make difficult for the "little people" of the world to launch their own successful businesses? No = -2, Probably Not = -1, Probably = 1, Yes = 2, Missing Value = 0.

The government should impose stronger safety regulations in factories, job sites and workplaces. Disagree = -2, Somewhat disagree = -1, Somewhat Agree = 1, Agree = 2, Missing Value = 0.

---

[a] The alpha reliability coefficients for the Business Regulation index are as follows:

Car accident data: alpha = 0.6772
Prescription drug data: alpha = 0.6472
Accounting data: alpha = 0.7130

Lawsuit Index (Respondent's answers to the following four questions are summed and then re-scaled to range between 0 and 1.)[b]

I become upset when I hear that a person in my community began another needless lawsuit. Disagree = 2, Somewhat disagree = 1, Somewhat Agree = -1, Agree = -2, Missing Value = 0.

Do you believe that the increasing number of lawsuits today is creating a crisis in this country? No = 2, Yes = -2, Missing Value = 0.

Do you believe that jury awards in lawsuits tend to be excessive? No = 2, Yes = -2, Missing Value = 0.

Do you believe that large corporations that have done nothing wrong are often sued simply because they have "deep pockets"? No = 2, Yes = -2, Missing Value = 0.

---

[b] The alpha reliability coefficients for the Lawsuit Attitudes index are as follows:
Car accident data: alpha = 0.6586
Prescription drug data: alpha = 0.5993
Accounting data: alpha = 0.6145

Index